Innovative Machine Patchwork Piecing

Hettie Risinger

Innovative
Machine
Patchwork
Piecing

Sterling Publishing Co., Inc. New York
Distributed in the U.K. by Blandford Press

Library of Congress Cataloging in Publication Data

Risinger, Hettie.
  Innovative machine patchwork piecing.

  Includes index.
  1. Patchwork.   I. Title.
TT835.R56   1983   746.9'7   83-4665
ISBN 0-8069-5486-8
ISBN 0-8069-5487-6 (lib. bdg.)
ISBN 0-8069-7700-0 (pbk.)

Edited and designed by Barbara Busch

Second Printing, 1984

Copyright © 1983 by Sterling Publishing Co., Inc.
Two Park Avenue, New York, N.Y. 10016
Distributed in Australia by Oak Tree Press Co., Ltd.
P.O. Box K514 Haymarket, Sydney 2000, N.S.W.
Distributed in the United Kingdom by Blandford Press
Link House, West Street, Poole, Dorset BH15 1LL, England
Distributed in Canada by Oak Tree Press Ltd.
% Canadian Manda Group, P.O. Box 920, Station U
Toronto, Ontario, Canada M8Z 5P9
Manufactured in the United States of America
All rights reserved

CONTENTS

ACKNOWLEDGMENTS

It is a rare thing when anyone stands completely alone in any endeavor. The writing of this book has, by no means, been one of those occasions. Throughout this entire experience, my husband has given his constant encouragement. Whenever he could do so, he relieved me of tasks which are usually my responsibility in order to free my time so that I would be able to meet deadlines in the schedule. Without his support in these and other ways, I am sure that this book would never have come into being. My appreciation for this is as unlimited as was his caring and his sharing of the experience in this way.

Betty Hartman, who typed the manuscript, graciously adapted her schedule to my needs. I am sure that she must have set aside her own plans frequently in order to push through chapter after chapter on time.

Gladys Hoffman, Ruth Gritzbough and Betty Reami gave generously of their time to make the "Counterpoint Whirlwind" quilt which appears on the cover of the book.

Jim and Connie Brown were very willing helpers with some of the drawings in the book.

Sharon Sodergren took care of the correspondence as needed, though she has a busy schedule of her own.

Many thanks to each of these people for expressing their friendship in such beautiful ways.

To my husband,
William Oliver Risinger

1

The Piecing Process

The making of a quilt is divided into two major processes: the piecing and the quilting. This book is concerned with the first of the two.

If you are already involved in the piecing of quilts, you have learned some methods for doing this. It is not my purpose to ask you to forget what you have learned. Instead I suggest that you may want to add some or all of these new methods to those you have been using. It is important, however, not to let your present habits prevent you from being open to other information which could be useful to you.

One of my aims is to help the piecer develop a larger selection of piecing methods from which to choose in the variety of situations, which arise while piecing patchwork patterns. Knowing more than one way of handling any given situation in piecing is a little like knowing several words with similar meanings. In each situation you can choose the one which works best. Therefore, the more versatile a person is in piecing, the easier the process becomes and the more accurate and refined the workmanship will be.

If you are a beginner, these methods are an excellent place to start, for they are easy to learn and to use, and they are time-saving. All this is especially encouraging to a beginner because it is nice to see good results occur quickly. Many of my students who work full time and manage a home as well have completely finished a quilt (even king size!) in two weeks. Being enrolled in a class was,

of course, strong motivation for achieving this. They could not have done so, however, with traditional methods. With these innovative methods it is possible to piece an entire top in a day if the pattern is a simple one.

The piecing methods usually used in patchwork are based on as much tradition as many of the patterns that are made. A template is made for each piece. It is used to mark individual pieces on the fabric. These are then cut out one at a time with seam allowances added beyond the marked shape, which is the exact size and shape of the finished piece. Many hours—even days—can be required for this process which many still insist is the only way to make the accurate pieces which, of course, are a basic essential to good piecing.

Once the cutting is finished, the pieces for a block are laid out in the pattern and the piecing begun. In blocks of numerous pieces, the pieces are stitched into units or sections, which eventually are joined together to complete the block. After that the process is repeated until enough blocks have been made for the entire top. The blocks are then set together in whichever way the quilter has chosen, and finally the top is finished and ready for quilting.

No one who has looked at quilts made this way can say that the method is not successful when followed with skill and patience. At the same time, no one can say that it is not very time-consuming.

A great deal of satisfaction can be experienced as the piecer watches block after block accumulate, sometimes laying them out in setting order to see how the top will look when it is finished. The careful stitching of narrow seams is not a thing to be rushed, so the piecer develops a steady rhythm of working and watching the blocks grow piece by piece. This requires and encourages relaxed muscles, so that the piecer who enjoys this type of work finds the tensions of the day slipping away as the fingers ease into their well-trained habits. There is a gentle pleasure to be found in the feel of soft cottons and the joy of working with lovely colors and the interesting relationships of shapes.

If you feel this way about the hand-piecing of a quilt, I would never tell you to change your ways. The time you would save by doing so is not likely to be as valuable to you as what you experience when working this way.

Not everyone experiences those same satisfactions when hand piecing, however. Some persevere through the piecing until ready for the quilting, and when the quilt is in the frame their pleasure begins. Another group does not have the time to piece by hand even if they would like to do so. Still others dislike handwork though they love beautiful quilts and want to be involved in making them by machine.

Remember that the machine has been used for piecing quilts since its introduction before 1850. Jonathan Holstein says in his book *The Pieced Quilt* (Galahad Books © 1973) that about half the quilts he has seen, dating from 1860 on, were pieced on the machine. Over one hundred and twenty years of use for this purpose should qualify it as a traditional tool!

There are numerous people, therefore, who have needed quick and easy ways of piecing quilts, ways that are at the same time accurate and produce attractive results. Various ways have been found to answer these needs. Often several people working in separate places find the same solution to one or another part of the problem. Sometimes more than one good method for the same construction is found. However it happens, the ideas accumulate because the need is growing and interest is high. Be assured that

a great deal of skill is required for making fine quilts by machine. I have yet to see the machine that can produce them without well-trained hands to guide and control the machine and the fabrics. The same abilities are required to work with colors and design and to perceive concepts as those employed by the handworker.

Though I enjoy doing various types of needlework, and though, when doing these things, I experience the same pleasures and satisfactions mentioned above, my interests and needs have also led me to do a great deal of machine work. I began to make simple garments before I started school and have sewn for myself and my family throughout the years since then, improving my skills through formal education as well as through learning to solve sewing problems on my own as they developed.

It was natural, then, that I turned to the machine when I began to piece quilts. It was equally natural that I sought my own methods for this type of sewing, since at that time almost nothing was printed on the subject. This is not to say that I have not learned from others as time passed. As more information has become available, however, I have not been restricted by what I have read or seen, but have continued to pick and choose from it and to find my own solutions as situations presented a need.

It is regrettable that I have not kept some sort of record over the years of the ideas accumulated from other sources and those I have developed personally. This is not something that one does, usually. There was no way of knowing that I would someday be writing books in which I would be very pleased to give credit where credit is due. Quilters are traditionally very sharing people, however, so I hope that those from whom I have learned are pleased to see their ideas passed along in this way even though I do not now know where to give the credit. It is in the spirit of sharing that I add my ideas to theirs for your benefit and for those you may be inspired to help.

The more I become involved with quilters and quilting the more I become aware of a chain of sharing which continues from generation to generation. To me, this quality of spirit is as real and important an expression of the personality of those who have it as are the quilts which they produce. I find that these are the same people who are always glad to share a recipe or lend a helping hand. It is the same spirit of supporting and encouraging one another that enabled early settlers to survive the difficult times in which the American patchwork quilt was born. It developed as that same spirit carried the quilts and the quilters to new territories and finally helped to build a nation. The history has not all been admirable, but this spirit has been a shining, guiding strength throughout.

Patchwork patterns, whatever their source, and the methods of piecing them necessitated the use of certain materials and equipment. It is appropriate to include here information about them, which I have found helpful.

Scarcely any type of fabric has escaped being used in quilting in one way or another. This is particularly true in contemporary works which were not intended for the usual uses of quilts and quilted pieces. Though these works may be objects of beauty and creativity, and though the methods in this book may be very useful in their construction, they are a special kind of quilting. The more general field of patchwork piecing usually turns to a more limited range of fabric choices.

These fabrics are usually cottons or blends of cotton and synthetic fibres. They are of the weight usually found in shirts, blouses and some dresses—fabrics such as calico, muslin and broadcloth. They should be fairly closely woven and of a quality to wear well. Used fabrics or portions of garments which have not been worn thin are also suitable, though some of the time-saving methods in this book apply best to pieces which are not too small.

Good quality 100% cotton is favored by many piecers because it wears well and is easy and pleasant to work with. They also feel it is more "traditional," when actually what is traditional is to use whatever is available and does not present too many problems in piecing.

Most cotton-blend fabrics work very well in most piecing projects. A few tend to ravel more than 100% cotton, however. This can be a nuisance when working with very narrow strips and segments such as are used in Seminole piecing. Some fabrics of blends are quite soft, which is very pleasant to feel, but can create problems when piecing narrow strips, especially if this fabric is stitched to 100% cotton. (See the comments on this subject with "Sarah's Choice" Pattern 85.) In most cases no problems will develop, but if you have trouble because of the softness or ravelling you might try spray starching. It is not likely that you will discover this kind of problem until after the pieces are cut, which is a little late. I would suggest, therefore, that soft fabric be spray starched (not heavily) in the process of ironing.

All washable fabrics should be laundered before they are cut. Several good reasons reinforce this practice. There is always the chance that even the best fabrics will shrink lengthwise and/or crossways. Laundering will eliminate the problems which this would cause. It will also remove any excess dye from the fabric as well as any sizing used by the manufacturer.

Wash and dry by machine, using the methods appropriate for your particular fabrics. Use water as hot as your fabric will tolerate to help in the shrinking and the removal of dyes and sizing. If the fabric is of a deep color there is always a chance of its bleeding in the wash. Test this by holding the fabric under very hot water and then squeezing out the water or letting it run on a white surface. If there is only a very pale color it is likely due only to excess dye which will be removed in the first washing. You may want to wash the fabric separately, however.

If there is definite color in the water from this test, or if there is still bleeding after the fabric has been washed once, it is best to set the color. Two methods may be used for this.

The first is less trouble so it is worth a try even though it may not work in some cases. Simply fill the washer with the hottest water and add a cup of white vinegar and the usual amount of detergent. Launder the fabric separately.

If there is still bleeding of color after this

procedure, then the second method is a sure success. Add a cup of white vinegar to each gallon of water in a large vessel made of non-porous material, such as enamel or stainless steel (I use the liner for my electric roaster). Aluminum will *not* do. Bring the solution to a boil and immerse the fabric in it while it simmers for about ten minutes. You must keep shifting and pushing the fabric down into the water as it simmers because steam keeps forming under it and lifting it out of the solution.

The same solution can be used for fabrics of various colors. It becomes a strange dark color after boiling red, yellow and blue fabrics, but the colors of the fabrics are not changed by this.

Just a word about ironing. Improper ironing of the fabric can cause problems from the beginning and throughout the piecing process. The old way of dampening the fabric ahead of time and letting it set for some time or overnight is best because the moisture will be more evenly distributed. Wetter spots, when ironed, tend to stretch more than the surrounding areas. This pushes the threads of the weave out of place.

Iron with the correct temperature, moving the iron with even strokes back and forth along the lengthwise threads of the fabric. Iron a single layer at a time.

Pressing is better than ironing when pieces have been stitched. The most carefully and accurately sewn pieces can be pushed out of shape with forceful ironing. Dampness at this point only increases the possibility of this. Handle your piece with the respect it is due by carefully pressing and gently encouraging the seams and pieces in the way they should go. Dampness may help, however, in a situation where it is necessary to reshape a badly ironed piece or area.

Another difficulty which sometimes occurs in the process of piecing is the necessity to take out some of the stitching. Everyone has encountered the need to rip while sewing. When dealing with ¼″ (.6cm) seams, however, more care must be taken than with wider ones. If you have not learned this way, it is well worth a try, for it is as fast as any other and does not damage the narrow seams

or the fabric at the stitching line. You will want to remember it also when working with delicate fabrics such as silks, velvets and sheers.

It is quite simple. Just slip the point of your ripper (one of the small types is best—be sure it is sharp) under every fourth or fifth stitch and cut the thread. When this has been done all along the area where it is needed, pull the thread on the other side of the fabric. It will come out easily leaving the fabric in good condition.

Now that you have learned how to take out stitching let us discuss putting it in. I feel that ¼″ (.6cm) seams are quite adequate for piecing. Wider seams are more bulky and require more fabric (you would be amazed how this can add up). The traditional ¼″ (.6cm) seam has survived through years of use even when it was stitched by hand. Surely with small machine stitches it is even longer lasting than before.

When machine piecing, I set my stitch length for 12–14 stitches to the inch. This way the stitches are strong and close enough together so that they will hold the pieces without the need for backstitching or tying the threads at the ends of seams. This is essential for chain-sewing convenience. Smaller stitches are also easier to guide accurately.

On the rare occasions when it is desirable to backstitch, turn the wheel by hand so that the thread uptake bar has reached its highest position and has just started back down. At this point backstitching can be done without creating a pucker from changing the direction.

If your seam puckers, it is not from using small stitches but because either the top or the bobbin tension—or both—is too great. If one thread has too much tension, it is likely to break. If one or both threads have too much tension they can create enough pucker on a long seam to change the length of the seam noticeably. I have seen a seam shortened as much as an inch in a yard by this condition. Think what could happen along the border seam of your quilt because of this. It is important that such a condition be corrected.

I have known machine repairmen to insist

that having both thread tensions tight but balanced makes a stronger seam. Whether this is true or not, if enough puckering occurs so that it is at all noticeable I contend that it is not a good seam. In any case it is not a seam which I will accept from my own machine.

When I take my machine for its annual check-up I always carry along scraps of calico and delicate fabrics (the ones most easily affected by tight tension). I always try the stitching on these fabrics and if it is not to my liking, I insist that it be adjusted so that it is, for I know that my machine *can* be adjusted so that it makes a balanced stitch which does not pucker in the least. If it does not do this I would buy one that would.

Besides a machine in good working condition, other equipment is needed to help you achieve accurate piecing with the least possible effort.

Needles. Good needles are essential to good machine stitching. A worn or slightly damaged needle can cause problems of skipped stitches or threads pulled in the fabric. Use sizes 80–90 or 12–14 for stitching the types of fabric usually used for quilting.

Thread. The best thread to use is the one which works best in your machine. If just any thread will work well in your machine, then I would choose cotton thread for use with 100% cotton fabrics. I have no problem with the best quality cotton wrapped polyester threads and feel they are a good choice with blended cotton and synthetic fabrics or 100% cotton. There is some question in the minds of those who are involved in the preservation of quilts as to the wisdom of using synthetic thread with cotton for fear the thread will wear the fabric over a period of many years. We know that synthetics are strong and tough enough to dull our scissors, pins and needles, but they have not been around long enough for us to know what effects will occur when they are combined as thread and/or fabrics in a quilt.

It is known that 100% cotton fabrics and threads can survive a hundred years and more with limited use and proper care. If this is a concern of yours (and there is no reason it should not be) I suggest you use only those fabrics and threads. You will also want to read one of the books on the subject.

Grandma Harrison always said, "Fold your quilts wrong side out to protect the tops, but don't fold them neatly." That way the folds come at different places and do not develop into creases which eventually tear. She often folded the edges in, to protect them. She liked to air her quilts in the early morning before the sun was really out. She avoided cloudy days, however, because she said she got her worst sunburn on those days and felt the clouds must let through rays which would fade the colors of her quilts.

It is now being said that quilts should not be stored in plastic bags because these keep out the air and because the chemicals from which they are made might damage the fabrics or colors.

Pins. Any kind of good quality pin which pleases you is all right to use. I do not recommend pins that are larger around than average, however, because they leave holes in the fabric. I have two favorite pins. One is a "long, extra-strength pleating pin" (#1074) made by Prym. It is size 20, which is 1¼" (3.2cm) long, and is very fine so that it slips through the fabric more like a needle. I use this pin for all my sewing except for heavy fabrics. Iris pins, which are from Germany, are similar but much more expensive. My other favorite is a long pin (also made by Prym, size 24) with a large white head. These pins are of average diameter. There is a similar pin, which is longer but heavier and should be avoided. Stretch and Sew sells an even longer white-headed pin, which is not too heavy. I use either one of these long, white-headed pins when working with heavier fabrics or when I add batting to my quilting project.

Scissors. Any good quality scissors are fine for this work, as long as they are in good condition and well sharpened. Experiment with your own scissors to see how many layers of fabric they will cut accurately and easily. The scissors I prefer are a brand called Ginghers. They are razor sharp and very well made. Naturally they are not cheap. I tell my students that cheap scissors are the most costly because they do not work well even to begin with. They cannot be sharpened successfully and must be replaced frequently. And they are always frustrating to use.

Take good care of your scissors by keeping the lint wiped off the blades, wiping them occasionally with a touch of oil and adding a drop of oil at the screw. But do not drop them. This will leave a nick in the blades where they crossed when they fell. Then they require sharpening.

Cutting Board. Cutting boards are available at all good fabric shops and departments. They are fine for protecting your tabletop, but that is not all: They help you to measure and to lay the fabric out square. They are an aid in straightening the end of the fabric (see Chapter 4). Strips and pieces can be pinned to the board to hold them in place while you match them or work with them in other ways. Until you have used a cutting board you cannot know how handy it can be.

Yardstick and Rulers. A good yardstick is very useful when marking strips across and along the fabric. It must be accurate (not all are) and have a straight edge (not all do). Test for this by laying the edge on a flat surface. I prefer metal ones (I have three lengths) which can be found at shops which sell art or drafting supplies. They are not only accurate and straight but are thin so that the marks are right at fabric level instead of ¼″ (.6cm) above it. This permits more accurate marking. They are more expensive, however, so you may not be ready to make that investment yet.

Triangles. If you want a triangle or two to use in drafting patterns, clear plastic ones are available in many places. I prefer the ones I bought at a drafting supply shop because they have tiny grooves at the edges which will not let ink run under the triangle when a pen is used as I often do when making drawings of patterns. You can use a triangle to draw truly "square" squares for the right angle (90°) is accurate. Get a 90° × 45° × 45° triangle and/or a 60°.

Ripper. I prefer the small one because it slips under stitches better.

Tape Measure. A good quality plastic or a fibreglass one is best because it wears indefinitely and will not stretch.

Thread Snipper. This is a very handy item when you get used to it, but it is not essential.

Markers. In most cases I mark pieces on the fabric with a fairly soft pencil (#1 or #2), which can be kept sharp. As I draw lines on the fabric to mark strips and pieces, I hold the pencil at a low angle to the fabric to keep the lead from pulling at the fabric (which can distort the line), and I roll the pencil between my fingers to help keep the pencil sharp. A sharp point is essential to accurate marking. Because of this I do not use markers with large leads, which break easily when sharpened. Many shops sell this type especially for use on fabrics on which a pencil mark will not show. For this use, I buy a pencil of the usual size with a white lead. These can be found at art or office supply shops, as well as at some quilt shops. They also can be kept very sharp.

There is a water-soluble marker which makes a fine enough blue line. More than one company makes them. Some are better than others. I use these sometimes, especially when the mark might show on the work. I simply mist the area with a water sprayer to remove the lines when I am finished.

Pencil lines can be removed with Spray 'n Wash® or with a solution of ½ tsp of Woolite in ¼ c of water. Test the fabric for fading before you use these.

Though pieces will be marked on the fabric, you will notice that no pattern pieces are printed for the patterns in Chapter 2. The designs are made by sewing together strips of fabric. These are cut crossways into segments, which are resewn to make the designs. No patterns are needed for this, but a special type of measurement is used. This will be explained.

For the usual types of patchwork patterns found in the rest of the book, pattern pieces are needed. Easy ways are given for drafting your own designs, as needed. This gives you the option of making your blocks whatever size you desire.

It is much better to draft your own patterns. Never fear, it is not that difficult. In the diagrams and instructions the information is given for folding or drawing lines on paper to form the shapes of the pieces needed. For drawn lines any smooth paper is satisfactory if large enough.

The best type of paper to use for folding is tracing paper. It is transparent, easy to work with and takes a good crease. Other lightweight papers are usable if you really cannot find the tracing paper, but some do not work well. You will have to experiment.

After the paper is folded as directed, use a ruler and a sharp pencil or pen to mark accurately around each piece needed. Some of these pieces can simply be measured. Then these measurements, with seam allowances added, are used to mark the pieces directly on the fabric (instructions in Chapter 4).

For some pieces a template is made to use in marking the fabric. For these pieces draw the shape or trace it exactly from the folded paper lines. Add seam allowances all around and transfer the shape to sandpaper, stiff cardboard or template plastic. Use it *as directed* in Chapter 4 to mark the shapes on the fabric. The method described for using the template may not be the same as you have used before. This way is faster and easier than the usual way.

Unit Measurements

For some designs no patterns need to be made. Measurements are given with the diagram instead. Throughout the book this type of measurement is used. I call them unit measurements because the measurements are given in units rather than in inches or centimetres. This is a very versatile way of indicating measurements because you can use it to make the pattern any size you want.

It is like the measurements for the solution of vinegar and water suggested above for setting colors in fabrics. I said to use one cup of vinegar to each gallon of water. Since you know that a gallon of water is 16 cups, the instructions could have read "use 1u of vinegar to 16u of water." In this case 1u would equal 1 cup. It could just as well have equalled 1 tablespoon if only a tiny amount of the solution were needed, or it could have equalled 1 quart for a large quantity. We are accustomed to putting one scoop of detergent to a washing machine of water or a certain number of tablespoons of bleach for each gallon of water. These are measurements which allow you to mix up any *quantity* needed and still keep the *proportions* of each ingredient the same.

Unit measurements, as applied to quilting, work the same way. If the diagram says a piece is 1u wide and 3u long you can let 1u equal any amount you need to make a pattern the size you desire. For example, suppose you want to make a "Rail Fence" block. The measurements for one strip or piece of this block are 1u wide and 4u long because four strips of equal width are pieced together to form the block. If 1u = 1″ (2.5cm) then 4u = 4″ (10.2cm) so your piece will be 1″ × 4″ (2.5 × 10.2cm) and the block would then be 4″ square. If 1u = 2″ (5.1cm) then 4u = 8″ (20.3cm), so the pieces would be 2″ × 8″ (5.1 × 20.3cm) and the block 8″ square.

But suppose you do not want your block to be either of those sizes. You want a 9″ (22.9cm) block. You know the size block you want and you know that there are four equal strips across it. What you need to know is how wide to make the strips. You can, of course, draw a 9″ square and fold it in fourths crossways and then measure the 22.9cm square width of the piece. This way you would have drafted your piece by folding the paper square, which is fine.

On the other hand you could simply divide 9″ or 22.9cm (the block measurement) by 4 (the number of strips) and find that each strip is 2¼″ (5.7cm) wide and therefore 1u = 2¼″ (5.7cm)

Either way you find the answer, you must then add seam allowances to the measurements to find the size to *cut* the piece.

Suppose that you want to make a quilt of Pattern 24 as it appears in Chapter 5. In Chapter 3, unit measurements are given for this pattern. At the scale used by the Seminoles, 1u might equal ¼" (.6cm). A study of Set *a* would then tell you that the top strip is ¾" (1.9cm) wide, the next two strips are each ¼" (.6cm) wide and the bottom strip is ½" (1.3cm) wide. You could go on converting the unit measurements for each set for the pattern into inches and then you would add ½" (1.3cm) to each measurement for seam allowance before you cut the strips and eventually made the blocks. They would be 1¾" (4.4cm) wide, rather small for your quilt.

A better choice for your quilt would be to let 1u = 1½" (3.8cm). Then for Set *a* the first strip would be 4½" (11.4cm), the next two strips would be 1½" (3.8cm) each and the last strip would be 3" (7.6cm). Those measurements would make a 10½" (26.7cm) block. Do not let the fraction disturb you. You do not have to divide it into equal parts for pieces or use it in any other way which might create difficulties. Just add ½" (1.3cm) to the measurement of each strip before it is cut and proceed to piece the quilt by the Seminole methods of sewing sets and cutting segments as described for the small-scale pattern. Be sure to mark segment widths on the wider pieces when marking the lines for the strips so that this will not need to be done later.

In Chapter 2, you will become more familiar with this way of indicating measurements for it is used with numerous Seminole patterns shown to illustrate the Seminole methods of piecing, described in that chapter. I think you will find them very practical to work with.

2

Basic Methods

Some time after the introduction of the sewing machine, the Seminole Indians developed a very innovative method of piecing patchwork designs on so small a scale that it would not have been practical without the machine, if indeed it could have been done at all.

These designs were pieced mainly for clothing, creating an effect of stripes. Though the Seminoles do not quilt these items, some of the patterns they use are the same as those often seen in patchwork quilts on a larger scale. Many other patterns can easily be adapted to quiltmaking and other quilted items.

In recent years quilters have begun to apply the very practical Seminole piecing methods to patchwork because they make the work faster and easier. In this section we will explore the Seminole piecing methods as applied to the various types of designs they use with the intent of adapting them to patchwork later. Numerous designs will be presented in such a way as to give a growing understanding of how each method builds on the previous ones and how additional variations can be made.

Although these patterns are given in a way that permits piecing them on the tiny scale used by the Seminoles, they can also be easily adjusted to any other scale such as that used by quiltmakers because of the adaptable type of measurements used here. For a full explanation of this, see the section on Unit Measurements in Chapter 1.

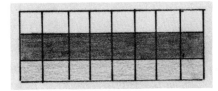

Illus. 1.

The pattern construction methods are based on sewing together two or more strips of fabric into what I call a "set" of strips. The sets are then cut into segments and sewn together again in different positions or combinations with the segments of other sets to form bands. All sorts of piecing ideas grow out of these basic beginnings to create many interesting and beautiful effects (Illus. 1–4).

Illus. 2.

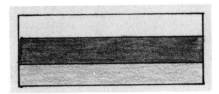

a. Set.

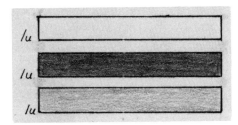

b. Set marked for segments.

Illus. 3. Set cut into segments.

Illus. 4. Segments sewn together into bands.

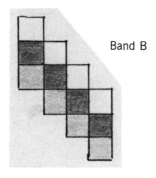

Band A

Band B

In this type of piecing as in all others, it is very important to measure, mark, cut and sew accurately in order to produce good finished work. This requires care. However, with these methods the work is not tedious, but progresses at a pleasing pace.

The strips of fabric used can be cut either lengthwise or crossways to the grain of the fabric. If the strips are to be cut lengthwise, lay the fabric out on a cutting board wrong-side-up and with selvages lying along a lengthwise line of the board. Measure and draw with a yardstick a line ¼″ (.6cm) from the edge of the fabric to eliminate the selvage.

If your strips are to be cut crossways, begin by laying the selvage along a lengthwise line and your yardstick along a crossways line of the board and draw a line near the end of the fabric (Illus. 6). In this case the selvages can be cut off later.

The measurements for all the patterns are given in units which can be used to figure the measurements and proportions of pieces for the pattern in any desired scale you plan to use to suit your project (see Chapter 1 for Unit Measurements).

Mark on the fabric lengthwise or crossways strips of the widths needed, each parallel to

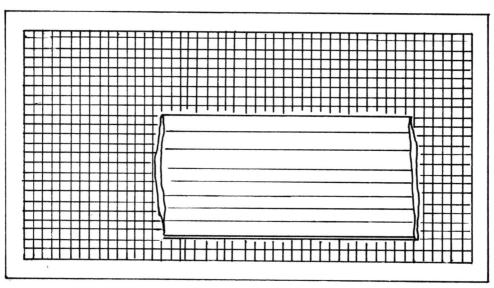

Illus. 5. Lengthwise strips marked on the fabric.

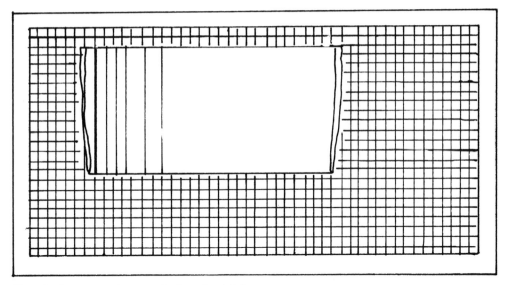

Illus. 6. Crossways strips marked on the fabric.

the first line drawn. (See Figs. 5 and 6). Mark as many strips as you need. Use a yardstick or a transparent ruler to make them even and accurate.

I use two different variations of the Seminole methods of cutting and sewing the fabric. Sometimes one is more convenient than the other.

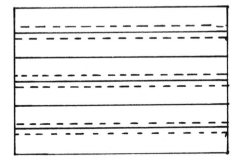

Illus. 7. Stitch strips before cutting.

1. When working with a very small-scale design such as the Seminoles use, I mark strips on the fabric as described. If two or more strips of different fabric *of the same width* are to be sewn together, I mark the lighter fabric on the wrong side, lay the two fabrics right sides together and pin along every other line. I then sew ¼″ (.6cm) from the line on both sides *before cutting the fab-*

ric. Next I cut along the lines and press the seam allowances (both in one direction) on the pairs of strips. For a design such as Pattern 2 or 11 I sew as many pairs of colors as I can. Then I join the pairs of strips to the desired width of the set.

When the set is finished, I press all the seam allowances in the same direction. Next I pin the edge of the set of strips along a line of the cutting board to make sure that it is lying straight. I make a template the width the segment is to be and use it to mark the segments on the fabric, taking care to see that each line is perpendicular to the edge or that diagonal segments are marked at the same angle.

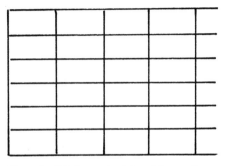

Illus. 8. Fabric marked for strips and segments.

2. When working with larger scale patterns such as for piecing quilts, I mark the width of the *strips* on the fabric as described above. Then I turn my yardstick or transparent ruler in the opposite direction and mark the width of the *segments* on the fabric. Next I sew the strip seams in the way described for the first method; then I cut the strips apart.

If no more strips are to be added to the set, I press the seam then hold the two strips together as stitched and cut the marked segments. (Pin if you must.) If another strip is to be added, I mark the width of the strip and length of pieces on the fabric also and pin it in place to the stitched strips before they are cut. I take care to match the segment marks as I pin. If another pair of strips is to be added to the first pair or to the three, I mark and stitch the second pair like the first then sew the two pairs together and cut the segments.

Marking the segments before sewing the strips is faster than taking the finished set of strips back to the cutting board to be marked with a template.

When strips of different widths are to be sewn together they must be cut apart before they are sewn. In this case, I will mark segments on the wider strip(s) to save having to do that later. As before, this marking is easier to do before the fabric is cut and sewn and saves time also.

In spite of all I have just said, you will find that the diagrams of the patterns show the marking of the segments on the sets of stitched strips. Do not be misled by this. The diagrams are drawn this way so that I can indicate the width of the segment in relationship to the set and can give the unit measurement for it. So wherever possible, mark the segments at the time that the strips are marked.

When cutting the strips of different widths which are not to be marked for segments, I usually fold the fabric in half lengthwise and/or crossways (carefully keeping the selvages together) to make as many layers as is practical. The wrong side of the fabric should be out. I mark only the top layer of the fabric,

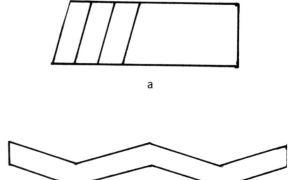

Illus. 9.

pin the layers and cut the strips. This marking must be done accurately. If the lines are not *exactly* perpendicular to the fold, zigzag strips will result. (See Illus. 9.)

With my Ginghers I can cut up to eight layers of fabric with ease and complete accuracy. For this reason, I do not hesitate to stack layers of different fabrics together when they are to be cut for the same size strips.

Illus. 10.

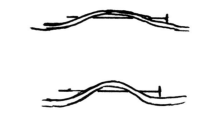

When pinning marked lines for cutting (especially when several layers of fabric are stacked), slip the pin in and out of the fabric layers at as flat an angle as possible to create as small a "hump" of fabric over the pin as possible. This hump tends to distort the cutting line and so can create problems particularly when very narrow strips or small pieces are to be cut.

Piecing diagrams are given for each pattern. Usually there will be several patterns for each type of piecing method shown. You will find also that the patterns are presented in an order which shows how one method of piecing builds on the previous one(s) to make the progressive learning process clear and easy.

When working with any of the patterns remember that two seam allowances of ¼" (.6cm) must be added to the measurements of the strips and segments after they have been converted from unit measurements into inches (or centimetres) to suit the needs of the scale of the pattern you want to make.

The simplest and easiest pattern presented is the first one. Patterns of this type are made by sewing two or more strips together to form a set of strips. The set is then marked into segments if this was not done before the strips were sewn. The segments are cut apart and chain-sewn together with every other piece in reverse position. Two matching sets can be pinned together with the bottom set of strips lying in the reverse order to those in the top set. (Only one layer needs to be marked.) When this is done, the first sewing of segments can be done before the segments are cut. Then continue the chain-sewing process to complete the band.

The diagram for Pattern 1 (Illus. 11) shows a sketch of each separate step of the construction of the band. Chain-sew wherever possible. Step 1 shows the two cut strips followed by Step 2 in which they are shown stitched together. Remember that the strips should be sewn before cutting whenever possible as described already.

Step 3 shows a template laid on the stitched strips as the segments are marked. This marking is done here if it was not previously done before the strips were sewn.

Step 4 shows alternate cut segments in reverse position. Remember that the first stitching of segments can be done as described before they are cut. The pairs of segments should then be chain-sewn to form the band as shown in Step 5.

In Step 6, edging strips have been stitched to opposite sides of the finished block. This step is optional and determined by the effect desired.

Illus. 11, Pattern 1.

a. Two strips.

b. Two strips sewn together.

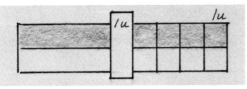

c. A template is used to mark segments on the fabric.

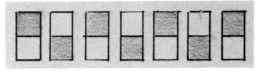

d. Segments arranged in alternating reverse positions

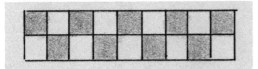

e. Segments stitched into a band.

f. A band with edging strips added.

Illus. 12, Pattern 2.

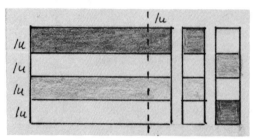

a. Set of four strips, with segments.

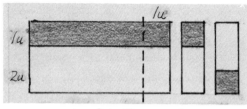

b. Band of segments.

Four strips are sewn together for the set for Pattern 2 (Illus. 12). They can be sewn in pairs before cutting. The pairs are then joined for the set.

The first sketch for this pattern and all those which follow combines all the information given in Steps 1 through 4 for Pattern 1. The second sketch shows the finished band.

Pattern 3 (Illus. 13) is made up of two strips which are wider than the segments. This creates a design of rectangles instead of squares. For variation, try the same idea with three or more strips.

Illus. 13, Pattern 3.

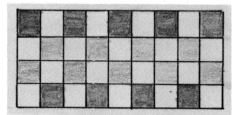

a. Set with segments.

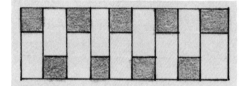

b. Band.

Strips of unequal widths are used for Pattern 4 (Illus. 14), making a design of rectangles and squares.

Illus. 14, Pattern 4.

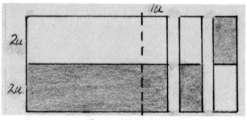

a. Set, with segments.

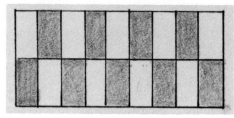

b. Band.

A set of two strips even wider are stitched together for Pattern 5 (Illus. 15), making it a variation of Patterns 3 and 4.

Illus. 15, Pattern 5.

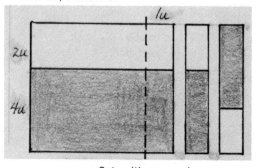

a. Set, with segments.

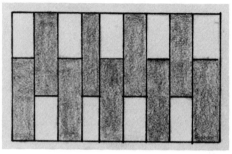

b. Band.

Two narrow strips and one twice as wide form the bases of Pattern 6 (Illus. 16).

Illus. 16, Pattern 6.

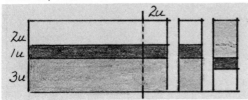

a. Set, with segments.

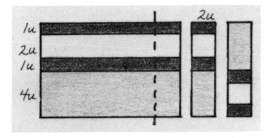

b. Band.

The segments of Pattern 7 (Illus. 17) are cut from a four-strip band.

The construction of Patterns 2–7 is virtually the same even though their appearance is different. They are only a few examples of what can be achieved by varying the number and widths of the strips and the width of the segments. The use of different color combinations for the same pattern lends additional change. With an understanding of these possible alternatives alone, you can make endless variations of patterns.

If you would like to pursue this interesting activity, work out your ideas on graph paper with color pencils or crayons, being guided by the sorts of sketches you see here. As you learn additional methods and types of patterns the scope of your creative thinking will be expanded. Some people find this to be the most enjoyable phase of patchwork.

Pattern 8 (Illus. 18) shows a different piecing of the segments of a single set of strips. Band 1 is shown pieced with the alternating segments reversed as before. For the new piecing, the segments must be cut before sewing, then the segments are shown joined (chain-sewn) in an off-set position so that the *bottom* seam of the two center strips of one segment is matched to the *top* seam of the two center strips of the next segment. The dashed lines indicate the seamline for Band 2, which is also drawn with edging strips to show the effect they give.

Sometimes it is desirable to have the segments slant in the other direction. This could be the case if two bands of the same pattern are to be used on each side of a jacket or blouse opening for instance. To achieve this, simply match the *top* seam of the two center strips of one segment to the *bottom* seam of the two center strips of the next segment and chain-sew. You will then have a band which is the mirror image of the one shown. In either case, the seams should be pinned exactly together and the stitching done before the pin is removed. "Tiptoe" the needle over the pin by turning the wheel by hand to spare the needle. Mismatched seams are just as noticeable as is the delightful effect of those which carry through as one stitching.

Other examples of this way of piecing the band are seen in Patterns 9, 10 and 11 (Illus. 19–21).

Illus. 17, Pattern 7.

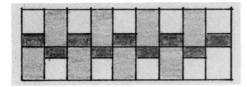

a. Set, with segments.

b. Band.

Illus. 18, Pattern 8.

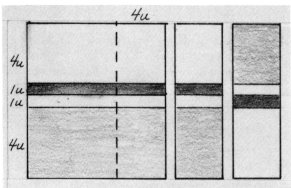

a. Set, with segments.

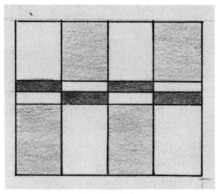

b. Band 1.

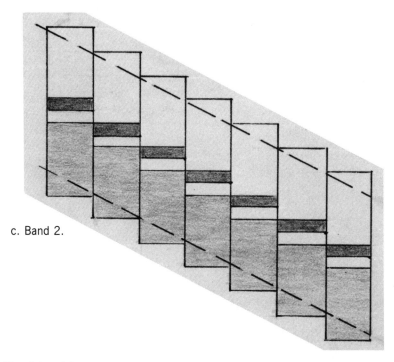

c. Band 2.

d. Band 2, with edging strips.

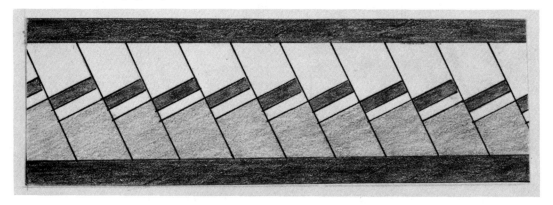

Illus. 19, Pattern 9.

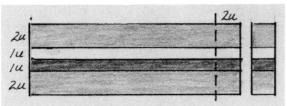

a. Set, with segments.

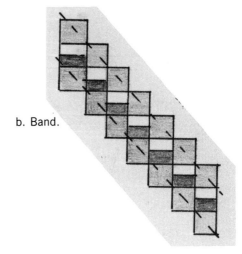

b. Band.

Illus. 20, Pattern 10.

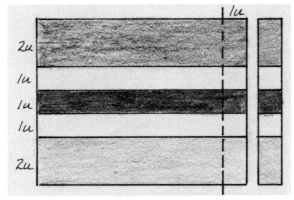

a. Set, with segments.

b. Band.

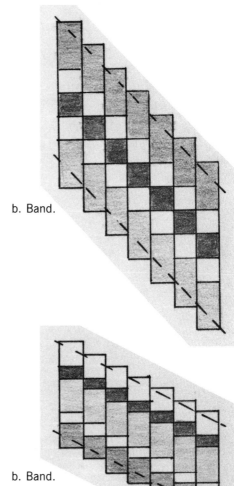

Illus. 21, Pattern 11.

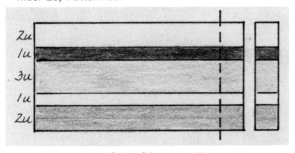

a. Set, with segments.

b. Band.

Illus. 22, Pattern 12.

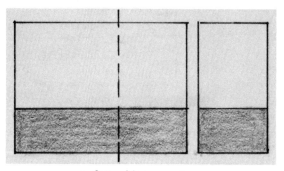

b. Long strip.

a. Set, with segments.

Step 1   Step 2   Step 3

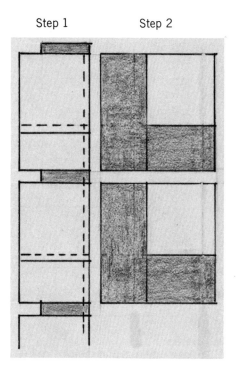

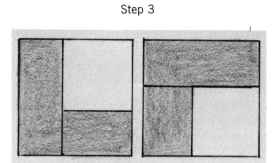

Step 1. Sew segments to long strip. This is strip-stitching.

Step 2. Cut strip to fit segments.

Step 3. Arrange in alternating reverse positions.

Step 4. Chain-stitch to make band.

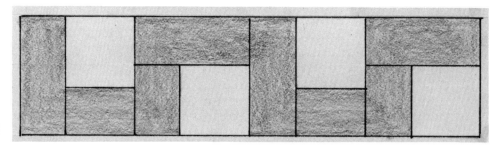

Step 4

In Pattern 12 (Illus. 22), something else is added. Instead of sewing the segments one to another, they are stitched one after the other to a long strip of fabric. This is strip-stitching. After this the strip is cut to fit the segments, which are then chain-sewn to form the band. Only one example of this is given here although others can be found. We will repeat the method with a different type of pattern, however.

With Pattern 13 (Illus. 23), we see the introduction of another idea, different from what we have done so far. In this case, two different sets of strips are sewn and cut into segments. The band is constructed by alternating a segment from first one set and then the other. Again, only one example of this piecing is used, but the introduction of the use of more than one set of pieced strips opens up endless possibilities for patterns. This can be expanded to include some very elaborate designs.

Piece two sets of strips as shown. Press the seams of one set so that they will lie in the opposite direction from those of the other set when the segments are sewn together. Mark the segments on one set. Pin the two sets together, matching the seams carefully where the segments will be stitched together. Sew the segments and then cut them apart. Continue by chain-sewing to form the band.

The ideas introduced with the last two patterns are combined in the construction of Pattern 14 (Illus. 24). Again two sets of strips are sewn, and one is marked for segments.' Twice as much is needed of Set *a*, than of the other so mark that one.

Press the seams as for the previous pattern (13). Lay the two strips together, pin, stitch the segments and cut them apart.

The segments of Set *a*, which are not used in this way are then chain-sewn to the segments of Set *b*, on the side opposite the first Set *a*, the segments thus forming squares.

Press the seams but do not cut the threads yet. First sew the squares to the long strip cut for this purpose (see Step 3 in diagram). This is done by the method introduced in Pattern 12, an idea much used in various types of patterns for fast piecing.

Cut the strip to fit the squares and continue by chain-sewing so that a strip separates each square in the finished band.

The method of sewing segments to a long strip is repeated in a slightly different way in Pattern 15 (Illus. 25). This time, only one set of strips is sewn and cut into segments. Half of these are stitched to one side of the long narrow strip called for. The other half are sewn to the opposite side of the same strip exactly in line with the first segments. Press the seams. Cut the strip to fit the segments so that squares or blocks are made.

Illus. 23, Pattern 13.

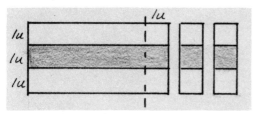

1. Set a, with segments.

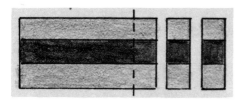

2. Set b, with segments.

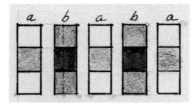

3. Alternating a and b segments.

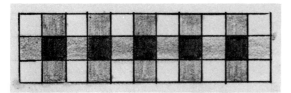

4. Band.

Illus. 24, Pattern 14.

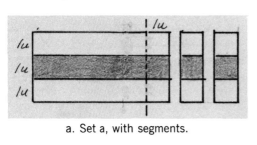

a. Set a, with segments.

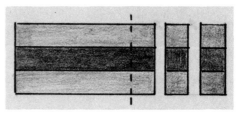

b. Set b, with segments.

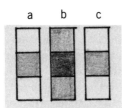

a   b   c

c. Order of segments.

d. Long strip.

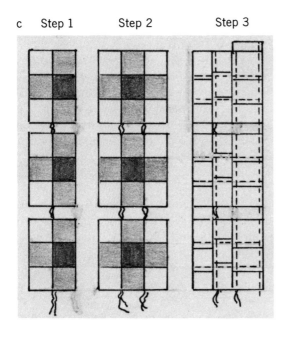

c   Step 1   Step 2   Step 3

Step 1. Segments a and b. Chain-sewn into pairs.

Step 2. Second segment a, chain-sewn to the pairs, to form squares or blocks.

Step 3. Blocks strip-stitched to long strip.

Step 4. Strip cut to fit blocks.

Step 4   Step 5

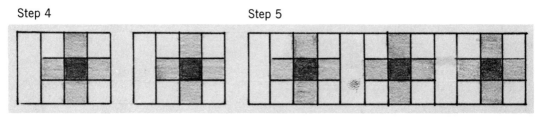

Sew these squares to the wide "setting strip" (my name for this piece), shown in the diagram, in the same way that the segments were stitched to the narrow strip. Next sew the opposite side of each square to a second setting strip the same width as the first. Press the seams in the same directions. Illus. 25, Pattern 15.

Now hold one wide strip, right sides together, under the square and use it as a guide to cut this strip to fit all the squares. Repeat the process with the second strip and you have a stack of "block-segments" (as I call them). Chain-sew these block-segments, carefully matching the seams as indicated in

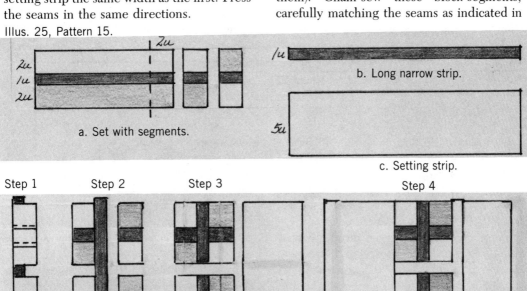

a. Set with segments.

b. Long narrow strip.

c. Setting strip.

Step 1   Step 2   Step 3   Step 4

Step 5

Step 1. Strip-stitch segments to long narrow strip.

Step 2. Add reversed segments to opposite side of strip.

Step 3. Cut strip to separate squares and strip-stitch to a setting strip.

Step 4. Strip-stitch second setting strip to opposite side of blocks to form block-segments.

Step 5. Chain-sew block-segments, matching seams carefully.

the diagram. Since the seams in the block-segments were all pressed in the same direction before the strips were cut, the block-segments can now be turned so that those to be matched lie in opposite directions for chain-sewing. The dashed lines in Step 5 indicate the edge seamlines for the band.

The methods shown so far are used for many beautiful patterns of squares which will look very familiar to the quilter since some of them are like, or very similar to, the quilt patterns they are used to. The difference is the method of piecing, which can be applied to large patterns as well as small. Among the following ones are several examples of this. It is the little squares or blocks, however, rather than the bands of which they are a part, that we will find of interest in later sections of the book. So let us look at a few more of them which are typical of Seminole designs.

In studying the diagrams you will notice that I have included one or more alternate choices of color-value placement. As in any patchwork, this can make such a difference in the appearance as to give the effect of a completely different design sometimes.

Pattern 16 (Illus. 26) uses three different sets of strips to form the design. Chain-sew them to make the block. Add setting strips to opposite sides and cut them to make the block-segments which are joined into the band.

Three sets of strips are also needed for Pattern 17 (Illus. 27). The construction of the band is the same as for Pattern 16.

Pattern 18 (Illus. 28) is very similar to Pattern 17. For this one, Set a is made up of five strips instead of three. The change makes possible several interesting variations. The same construction as for the others is used.

A slightly different twist is introduced in Pattern 19 (Illus. 29). The segment of Set a on the right side of strip b is placed in the reversed position to that on the left when the segments are chain-sewn. Otherwise the construction of the band is the same as usual. Reversing the segments when chain-sewing gives an interesting diagonal figure in the band. When set as in the first variation shown, where the setting strip is the same color as the light color in Set a the figure seems to float, unattached, in that color. If edging strips of the same color were added, the effect would be heightened. Longer setting strips would create the same effect.

An asymmetrical figure is formed by the segments of Pattern 20 (Illus. 30). The usual construction for bands of block-segments is used, however.

Another strongly diagonal figure is found in Pattern 21 (Illus. 31). The blocks can be set in either variation seen for Pattern 19. I don't know if I have ever seen the setting in Variation 2 used in Seminole work. Construct this pattern the same way as the others.

A little nine-patch is found in the center of both Patterns 22 and 23 (Illus. 32 and 33). Again, the difference is to be found in the strips for Set a. Pattern 23 is interesting in that it can have either a diagonal or a square appearance. This is achieved for Variation 3 by making the top and bottom strips of Set a the same color.

For Pattern 24 (Illus. 34) there is a variation in the block as well as in the way it is set. Block construction is the same as for other patterns of this type.

Now that you have had a chance to become thoroughly familiar with all the methods employed in constructing designs for bands made with block-segments, Pattern 25 (Illus. 35) should not seem too difficult. It is simply an elaboration of these same methods to create what I call a double-block pattern because it seems to be made up of two identical blocks which overlap at one corner. By following the diagram step by step you will find that it all works out very nicely. The challenge is well repaid by the beautiful results.

The pattern is divided into two parts for piecing. Begin with the familiar chain-sewing of the segments of the first three sets of strips a, b and c. Then join one segment of each set as in Step 1. Strip-stitch a narrow strip across the top of the segments and a setting strip across the bottom as in Step 2, and you have finished Part A. For each block, make two of Part A.

Chain-stitch segments of Sets d, e and f for the upper section of Part B. Make another section just like it for the lower section. Reverse this section and chain-sew a segment of Set g between it and the upper section to complete Part B. (See Step 5.)

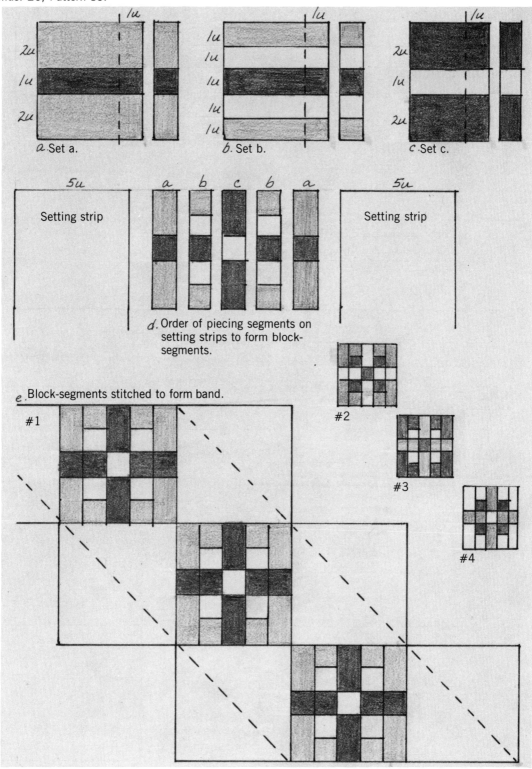

a. Set a. *b.* Set b. *c.* Set c.

5u — Setting strip

a b c b a

5u — Setting strip

d. Order of piecing segments on setting strips to form block-segments.

e. Block-segments stitched to form band.

#1

#2

#3

#4

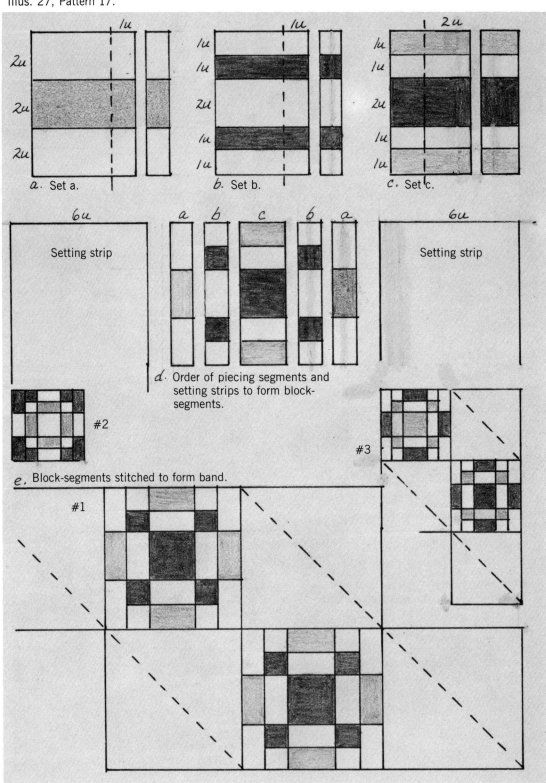

a. Set a.

b. Set b.

c. Set c.

Setting strip

a   b   c   b   a

Setting strip

d. Order of piecing segments and setting strips to form block-segments.

#2

#3

e. Block-segments stitched to form band.

#1

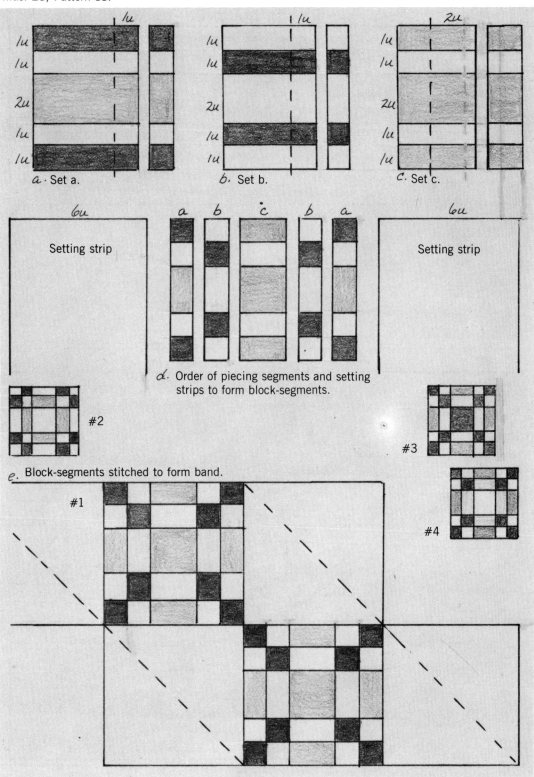

a. Set a.

b. Set b.

c. Set c.

Setting strip

a b c b a

Setting strip

d. Order of piecing segments and setting strips to form block-segments.

#2

#3

e. Block-segments stitched to form band.

#1

#4

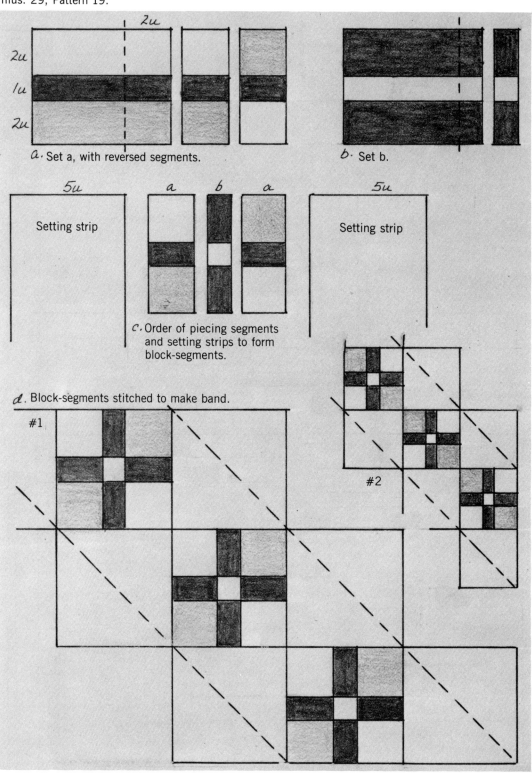

a. Set a, with reversed segments.

b. Set b.

c. Order of piecing segments and setting strips to form block-segments.

d. Block-segments stitched to make band.

Illus. 30, Pattern 20.

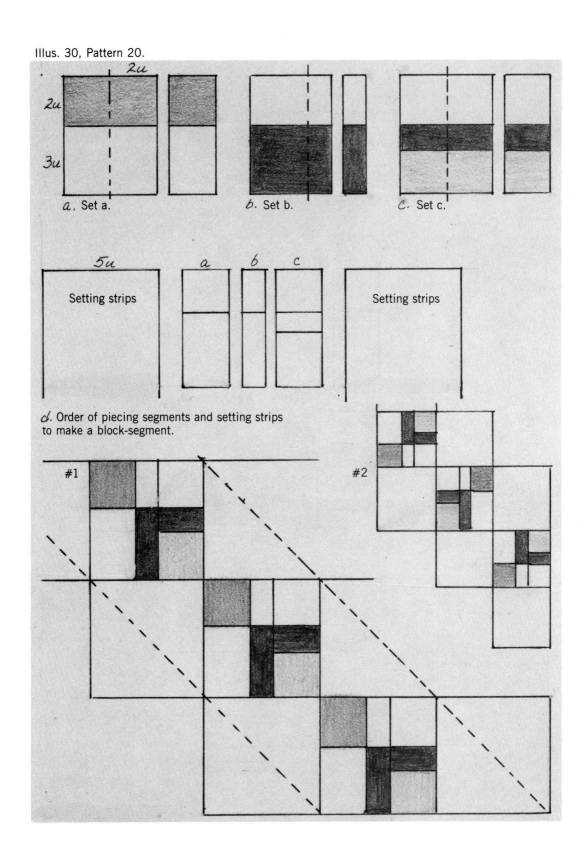

2u

2u

3u

a. Set a.

b. Set b.

c. Set c.

5u

a   b   c

Setting strips

Setting strips

d. Order of piecing segments and setting strips
to make a block-segment.

#1

#2

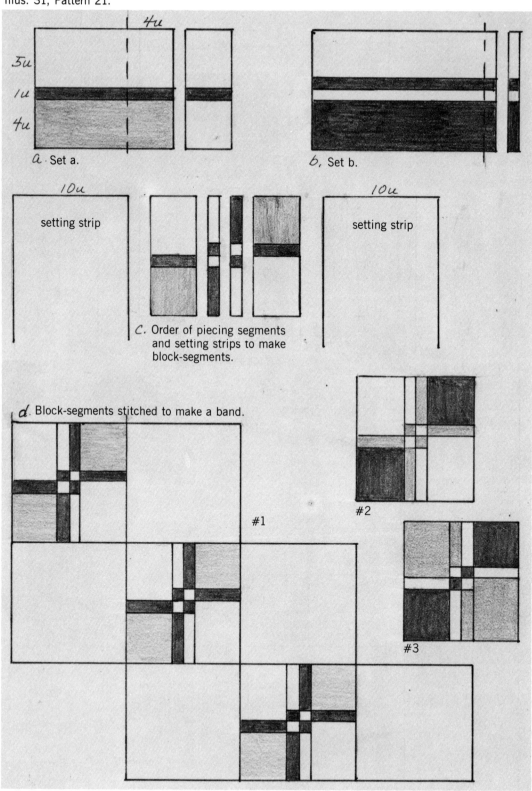

a. Set a.

b. Set b.

10u

setting strip

C. Order of piecing segments and setting strips to make block-segments.

10u

setting strip

d. Block-segments stitched to make a band.

#1

#2

#3

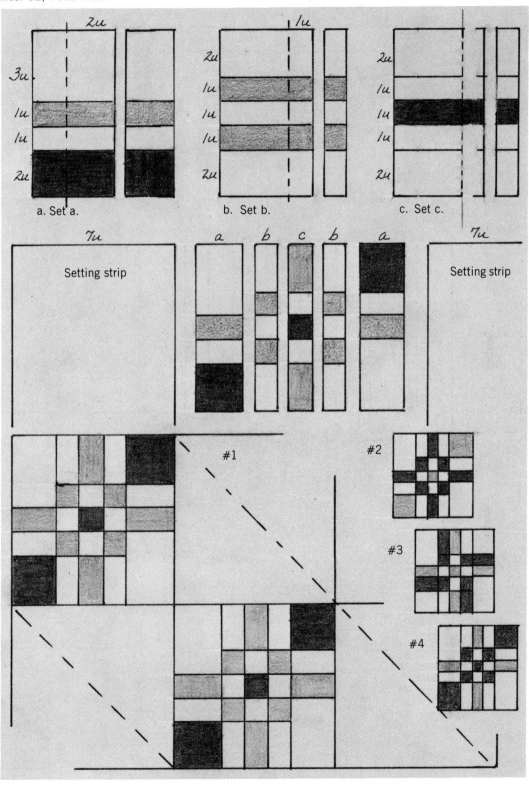

a. Set a.   b. Set b.   c. Set c.

Setting strip   Setting strip

#1   #2   #3   #4

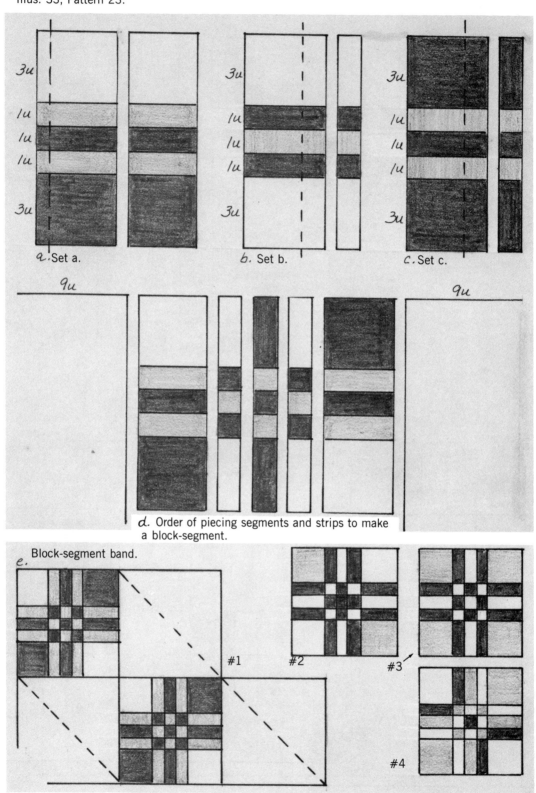

a. Set a. b. Set b. c. Set c.

d. Order of piecing segments and strips to make a block-segment.

e. Block-segment band.

#1 #2 #3 #4

Illus. 34, Pattern 24.

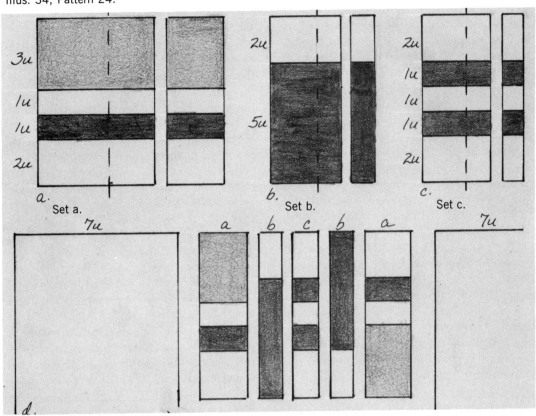

Set a. Set b. Set c.

Piecing segments and sets to make a band.

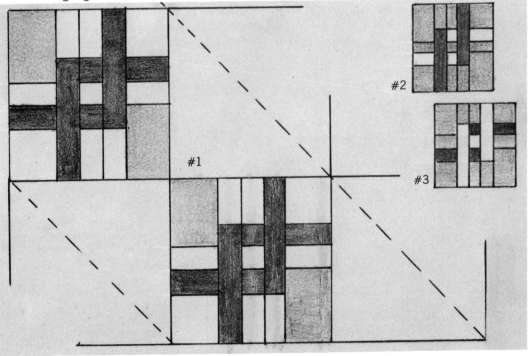

#1

#2

#3

41

All that remains is to chain-sew one Part A to a Part B. Then reverse the other Part A and chain-sew it to the opposite side of Part B. This completes the block. Strip-stitch setting strips to opposite sides of the blocks to make the block-segments for the band.

One more type of Seminole pattern is now to be considered. It is actually very similar to what has already been done and is a natural extension of them.

From the point of view of the quilter, the patterns which follow lend themselves best to use for borders. The methods permit the piecing of very intricate designs for this purpose, however, without the tedious work which would otherwise be required.

We will begin with a simple version and progress to a few which are more involved. As always, the first step is to piece a set of strips, cut it into segments and chain-sew them into a band. This time, however, the segments are cut on a diagonal instead of at right angles to the edge.

Each pattern is shown pieced in three different ways to make a different band. This type of thing can be done with many variations of pieced strips simply by cutting the segments at a 45° angle (or even a 30° or some other angle) instead of cutting them at right angles (90°) across the set.

For each pattern the piecing for Band 1,

Band 2 and Band 3 is the same. In each case start by marking the set with lines drawn at a 45° angle as shown. To make Bands 1 and 2 in which the segments slant in the direction shown, mark the right side of the fabric as shown. If you want the segments to slant in the other direction, mark the segments on the wrong side of the fabric or slant the marks in the other direction on the right side.

For Bands 1 and 2, cut the segments apart, pin them in the position shown in the diagram and chain-sew them to form the band.

For Band 3, two identical sets of strips are sewn. Mark the diagonal segments on one of them, pin the two together so that the seams match and stitch the segments ¼" from the marked lines before cutting them. The stitched pairs form a chevron design. Chain-stitch these chevrons to form the band.

In this section we have devoted our attention to learning the practical piecing methods developed by the Seminole Indians as well as some variations of them which increase their value in speeding and easing the construction of patchwork piecing. In the next section, we will be involved in exploring variations of patterns for use in patchwork designs.

Other methods for increasing the ease and speed of patchwork piecing will be found in the following sections where their use applies to what is being done at the time.

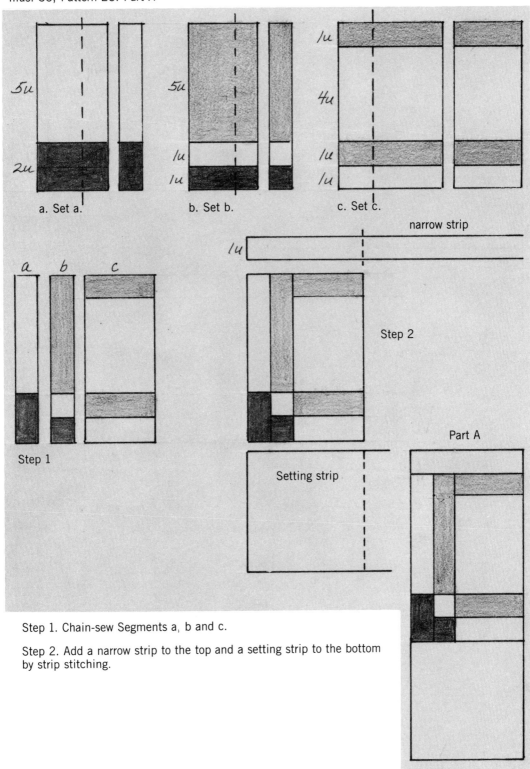

a. Set a. b. Set b. c. Set c.

narrow strip

Step 1

Step 2

Setting strip

Part A

Step 1. Chain-sew Segments a, b and c.

Step 2. Add a narrow strip to the top and a setting strip to the bottom by strip stitching.

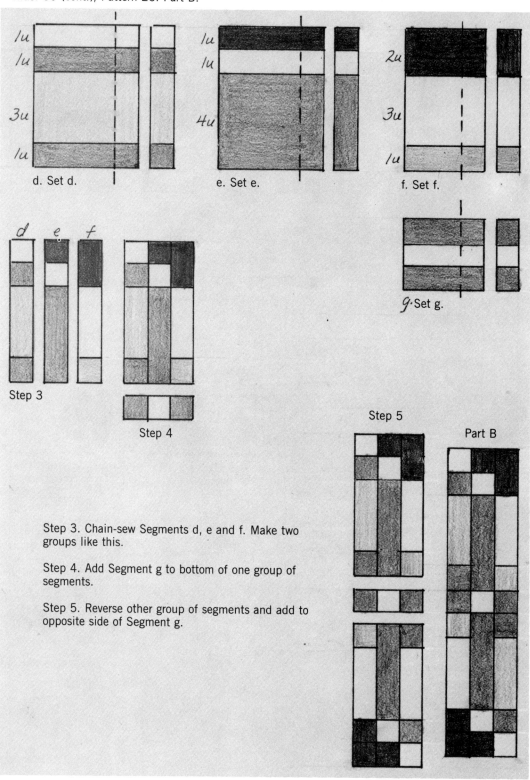

d. Set d.

e. Set e.

f. Set f.

g. Set g.

d   e   f

Step 3

Step 4

Step 5

Part B

Step 3. Chain-sew Segments d, e and f. Make two groups like this.

Step 4. Add Segment g to bottom of one group of segments.

Step 5. Reverse other group of segments and add to opposite side of Segment g.

Illus. 35 (cont.), Pattern 25, Completed.

Part A   Part B   Part A reversed

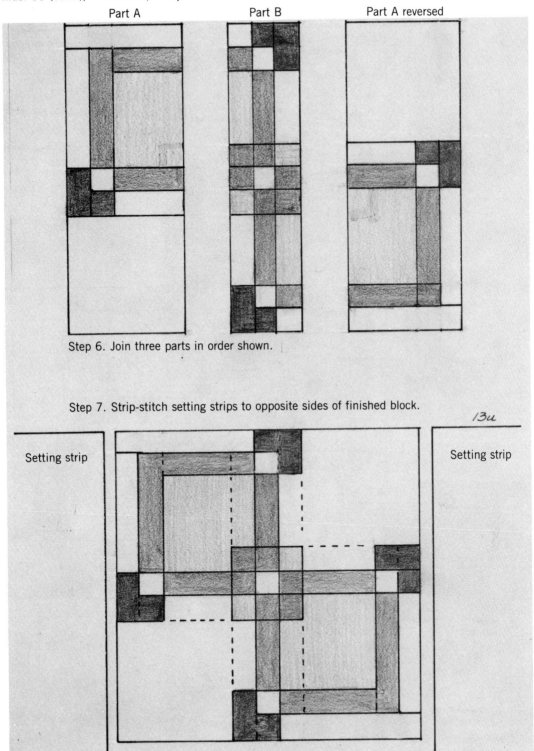

Step 6. Join three parts in order shown.

Step 7. Strip-stitch setting strips to opposite sides of finished block.

13u

Setting strip

Setting strip

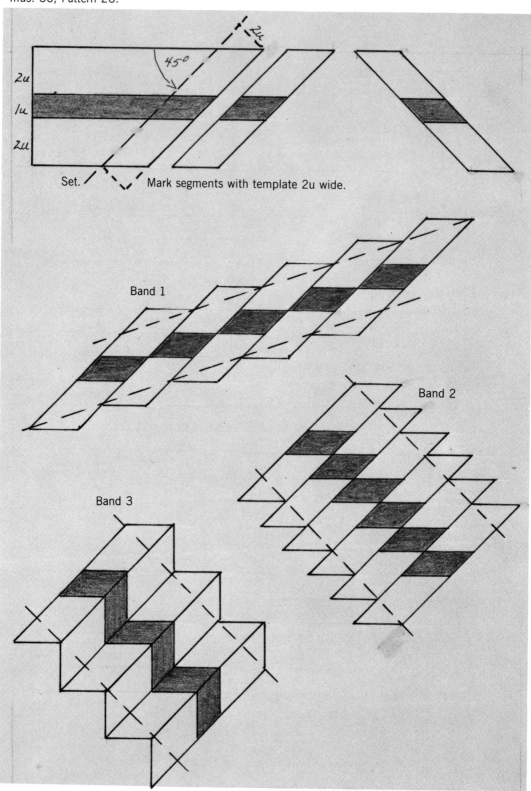

Set. Mark segments with template 2u wide.

2u
1u
2u

45°

2u

Band 1

Band 2

Band 3

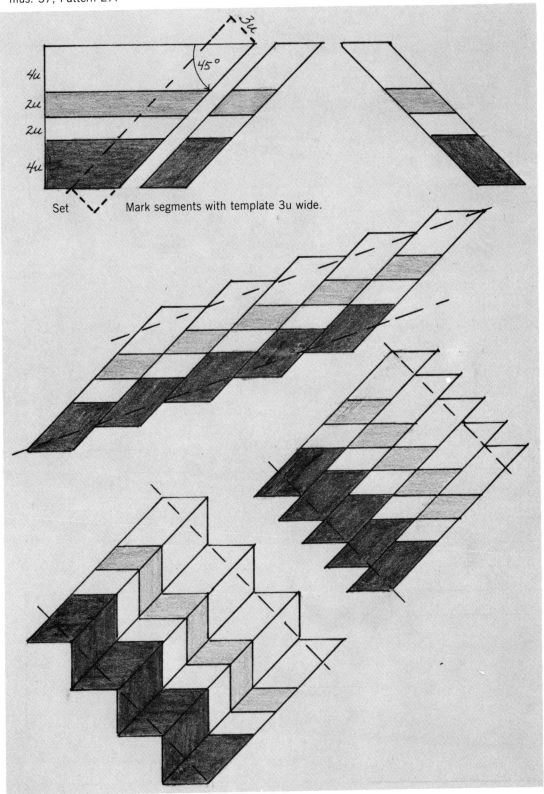

4u

2u

2u

4u

3u

45°

Set   Mark segments with template 3u wide.

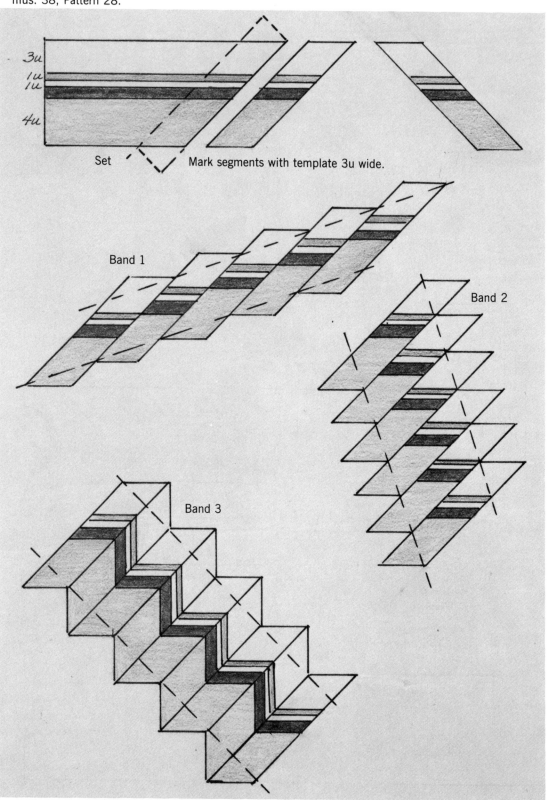

3u
1u
1u
4u

Set   Mark segments with template 3u wide.

Band 1

Band 2

Band 3

3
Designing Ways

In Chapter 2 we made a study of the piecing methods of the Seminole Indians, including some variations, which I prefer. We also worked with various types of Seminole patterns. Gradually I began to make suggestions about the possibility of varying the widths of strips and segments to change the patterns. Then I began to show differing choices of shading in the small pieces of a pattern to help you realize the possibilities for this in these patterns as well as in all types of designs.

Now we are ready to explore additional approaches to making patterns and variations. Though this is done creatively, I have avoided the term "creating" patterns because it is a questionable one. It is said that there is no such thing as an "original" design, that somewhere someone has already done it. This is probably more or less correct. Certainly I have had the experience often enough of drawing a design, which was new to me, and then coming across it, or one very similar, labelled "old patchwork pattern" or "a design from the Alhambra" or the like.

Quilters, like all others who work with patterns, have long been in the habit of making changes in known designs to suit their fancy thus "creating" variations and sometimes entirely different designs. They have also been quick to notice designs in other crafts and arts, which can be used or adapted for use, in patchwork. There is no reason why these things should not be done, which is just as well, for they will continue to be done—and

with much pleasure and success. So if the patterns you "create" in the process are not exclusively yours they will at least be new to you and you will have had the joy of discovering them for yourself. I feel that this is creative even though it may not produce something entirely original. It can be one path which leads to originality.

There are many other sources of pattern ideas than subdividing familiar patchwork patterns. A quilter soon learns to be aware of pattern sources almost as a reflex. Watch for grillwork of all types, tile floors (especially in old buildings), fabric in medieval paintings, photographs of the Alhambra and medieval buildings, patterns painted on pottery or woven into baskets and blankets, brickwork in old buildings (I found some interesting brick designs in Mexico), leaded windows with geometric patterns, plaid fabrics, geometric designs everywhere, patterns stamped on book bindings, border designs on all kinds of items. Some of these can be transferred almost directly into patchwork, others require some translation, and still others may simply supply an idea which can be adapted for piecing. The habit of being aware of patterns about you will, in itself, stimulate your ideas.

As you become increasingly acquainted with the patterns in this book you will not only be looking at all sorts of things for pattern ideas, but you will also be thinking about how these patterns can be pieced with these methods to save time and energy.

When working with the patterns in Chapter 2, we saw that the most basic element was the strip. We began with strips of fabric which were sewn together to make a set of strips. The "set," of course, is just a pieced strip. The set was cut into "segments" which were also a kind of strip. They were stitched together to make a "band" which is another way of saying strip.

In some patterns we made squares or blocks. These were pieced of segments (little crossways strips of the set) and then strip-stitched to setting strips to form what I call a block-segment because it is stitched together with others of its kind in the same ways that segments of the set are joined, and when this is done, the two form a band (or strip).

With all this in mind, it is easy to see why I think of this type of piecing as "strip-piecing." The methods, as has been said, can also be used to advantage for other types of piecing such as patchwork which is our main concern in this book.

In exploring pattern variations, it is important that we keep in mind this concept of working with strips and segments and of the methods used with them. The concept itself will be a foundation upon which ideas for patterns will grow—ideas which would not naturally develop within the usual concept of patchwork piecing.

I became aware of this when I first began working with Seminole patterns in preparation for teaching a class on the subject. I was already teaching a class which included Roman Stripe variations in the lessons. It occurred to me that sewing rectangular pieces together for Roman Stripe blocks and then setting these together to form either "Rail Fence" or "Windmill" was very similar to piecing strips together to make a set of strips and cutting it into segments which were then stitched together into various patterns.

Though I was certainly not the first one to discover this idea, it was new to me at the time. I became very excited over the potential for variety of design. I began at once to experiment on graph paper (or any scrap of paper handy when an idea came) with various Roman Stripe settings.

Following are numerous actual sketches I made while working with the idea. They are not very neat for I was, at the time, concerned only with getting ideas on paper. I certainly had no idea of anyone else ever seeing them. I am now adding pattern numbers to them for convenience as a reference. These sketches are selected to show the flow of ideas from one to another and where they led. During the time period covered by these patterns I did many other designs which are not included because they are not part of this particular branch of my thinking. Some of the other patterns are included in following chapters because they are related to them as one branch of a tree is related to the others though they do not lead in the same direction.

Since Seminole patterns are made on a very small scale (often ¼" (.6cm) wide strips, not including seam allowances), my first idea was to work at this scale. Very soon, however, I expanded my concepts to include work with wider strips and segments.

It is not surprising that these earliest experiments were related to Roman Stripe. Instead of four equal strips to make the block I used two narrow ones, each ¼ the width of the set, and joined the two middle strips in a single one ½ the width of the set. Later I saw a block like that in a book—so I wasn't so original after all. However, if I had not been working with this variation of the Roman Stripe block, I would not have designed the setting in Pattern 29 which I named "Stepping Stones Around the World" and made into a throw-size quilt.

I really got carried away with this little three-strip segment. My small graph pad went with me to meetings and waiting rooms. While others knitted, I drew little patterns. I even began carrying a soft eraser and small pencil sharpener to keep the sharp point I prefer.

From Roman Stripe I quickly progressed to using the segment in drawing nine-patch variations and from there I escaped into fantasy! That same little three-strip set was cut into segments of varying lengths for designs that became very elaborate indeed.

Illus. 39, Pattern 29. "Stepping Stones Around the World." See the variations of this pattern in Chapter 6.

With Patterns 35 and 36 (Illus. 45 and 46), something different began to happen which I didn't become aware of at the time because I was busy following my ideas and not wondering where they came from. I didn't notice that these are transitional designs. Pattern 35 is still a block, but it shows a hint of what could happen in Pattern 36 which is not a block. The strange thing is that something about the shapes formed in Pattern 36 caused my thinking to jump to Patterns 37 and then 38 (Illus. 47 and 48). Patterns 35–38 were a bridge between what I had been doing and what I began doing later.

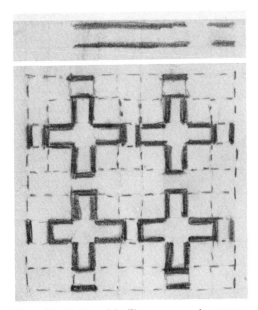

Illus. 40, Pattern 30. Three segments square.

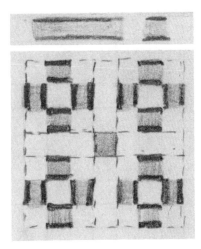

Illus. 41, Pattern 31. Seven segments square.

After a few more flights of fancy, I finally came down to earth with a few related designs shown in Illus. 49, Patterns 39–42.

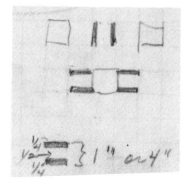

Illus. 42, Pattern 32. Eleven segments square.

It occurred to me one day that I was not really working with Seminole nor had I been for a long time almost from the first. It is true that in the earlier patterns I was sewing segments of pieced strips into patterns but the patterns were not Seminole. The patterns were patchwork. I was using strip-pieced segments in place of what would otherwise have been ordinary patchwork pieces. The segments of pieced strips were simply a way of making patchwork pieces different without adding to the difficulty of the piecing process.

Like someone happily chasing after a butterfly, I had followed my ideas into strange and interesting paths which reached out ahead of me intriguingly. It is not necessary that every path end in a design, fascinating to all who see it. It is gratifying that some are appreciated and enjoyed but important to enjoy the process so that the ideas continue.

You have seen the beginning development of one succession of ideas which sprang from my interest in Seminole patterns, and yet what I have said has been more of a history with very little said about how it happened.

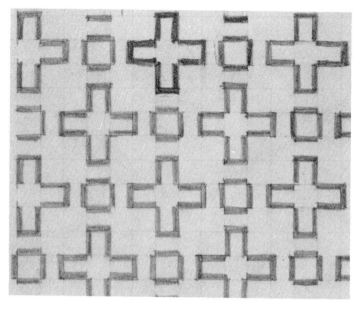

Illus. 43, Pattern 33.

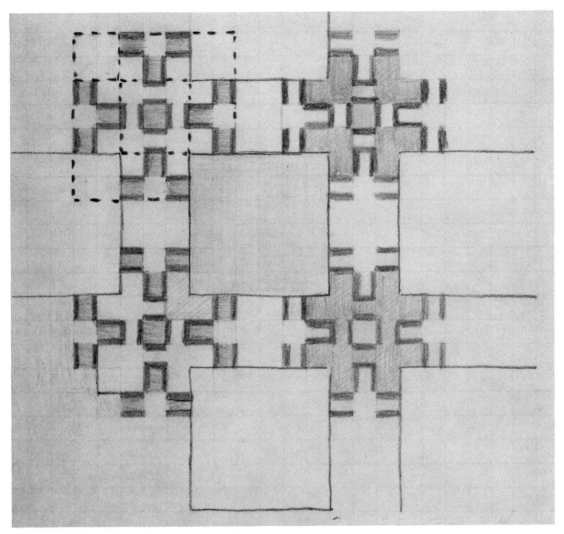

Illus. 44, Pattern 34.

My students ask about this. They say that after they have kept their eyes open to the many designs around them, as suggested earlier, they sit down with pencil and graph paper and still nothing happens. They ask how to develop what they have seen into ideas.

This is a very difficult question to answer and I think that this is because there is more than one answer. I think the answer is more or less different for each individual according to personal ways of doing things and of thinking things through.

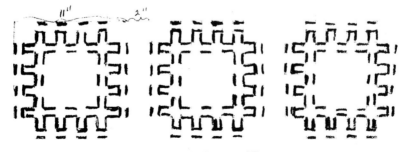

Illus. 45, Pattern 35

For me it does not happen when I am being determined and direct: "Now I'm going to sit down and draw some designs." It happens when I am relaxed and casual about it and a little playful. A touch of the feeling of adventure and anticipation and wonder and excitement are involved, if not at first, then at least very soon. It is an attitude similar to the one I might have if I were to say, "What a lovely day! I think I'll walk down to the creek and see if the leaves have started to turn." In that same way I say to myself, "I think I'll sit down awhile with my graph pad and see what happens." So I do. I don't usually begin with a preconceived idea unless it is one which came to me at a time when I wasn't free to do something with it and have therefore waited for this chance to work with it. Otherwise I sit and look at the paper almost as though I were waiting for something to appear there.

I may draw a few tentative lines the way a gardener might scratch gently at the surface of the soil to see if the seeds are beginning to sprout.

Presently the lines, or something in my mind, seem to suggest an idea. It likely will be something rather ordinary like "Nine-patch." But that's all right. It's a start; and it is amazing where "Nine-patch" can lead. So I draw "Nine-patch" and maybe another one beside it, or two or three rows of them. And then I begin to get an idea about subdividing some of the pieces so that the blocks work together to form an interesting pattern.

It doesn't matter to me whether the design is original or not. It matters that I am having a good time following the flow of my ideas as

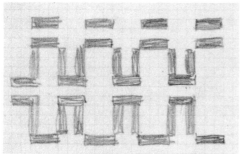

Illus. 46, Pattern 36.

Illus. 47, Pattern 37.

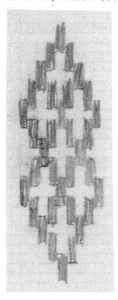

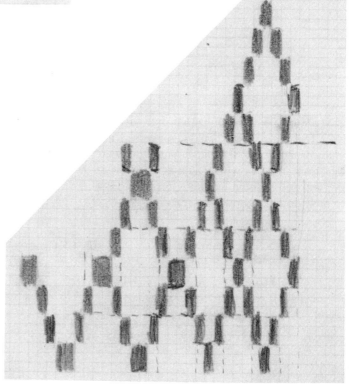

Illus. 48, Pattern 38.

Pattern 39

Illus. 49, Patterns 39–42.

Pattern 40

Pattern 41

Pattern 42

they come. That seems to be the sort of situation which brings them forth.

Pattern 43 (Illus. 50) is a good example of exactly what I have been describing. I was playing around with "Nine-patch." I drew a square of 6 × 6 tiny blank nine-patch blocks. Thinking of them more as a unit than as individual blocks, I began to shade in the little patches here and there in an allover pattern without regard to the lines of the blocks.

When it was finished I saw that the design divided naturally into two alternating blocks, neither of them nine-patch. A diagram for Pattern 43 is found in Chapter 4. I call it "Argyle."

Another time I began with a "nine-patch" (Pattern 44, Illus. 50), dividing the corner squares into little "four-patch" blocks. To this I added several more "nine-patches" set together with some setting blocks, somewhat

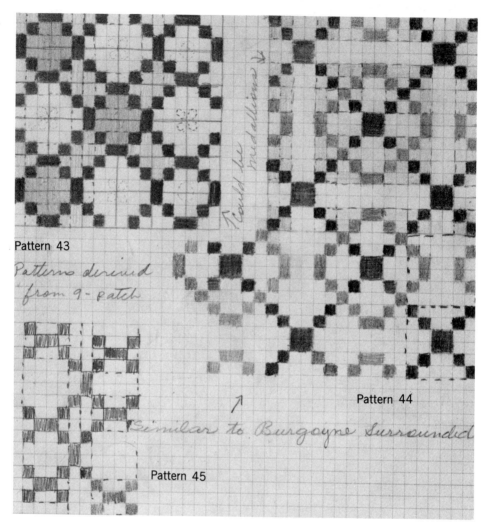

Within the illustration (handwritten notes):

Pattern 43

Patterns derived from 9-patch

Could be medallions ↓

Pattern 44

↑ Similar to Burgoyne Surrounded

Pattern 45

Illus. 50, Patterns 43–45 (left to right).

in the manner of "Single Irish Chain." Then I began to divide the setting block into patches by shading in four squares and two rectangles, finally adding shading to the "nine-patches." Tiny nine-patches are still a part of the design; but not the larger ones with which I began. The design reminded me of "Burgoyne Surrounded," and with that my time was up. I filed Pattern 45 (Illus. 50).

In the meantime I continued to work with "Nine-patch" variations, which often ended as something else, as well as various other things. Patterns 46–49 (Illus. 51) are some

which were done on a cold day in January. Each one is drawn in a larger square divided into 9 × 9 little squares.

The next day I began with Pattern 48 from that group. Because I had been working on a "Trip Around the World" to be used as a class sample, I surrounded the pattern with a border of small squares. Another border of tiny "Nine-patch" flowers was added. After that I added another medallion like the first one and the "Nine-patch" flowers became a lattice-type design with an extra pattern of squares around the flower where the lines

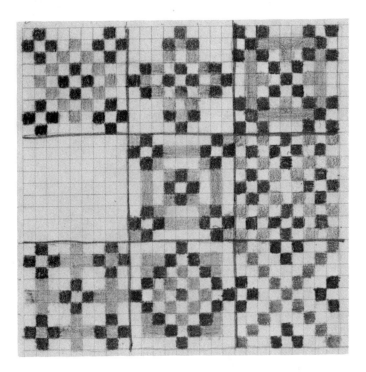

crossed. This one is Pattern 54, "Variation on a Square." (Illus. 52).

As before, when my imagination led me into fantasies, I finally wondered: "How would a person go about piecing a thing like that?" Then I began to see that the design could easily be divided into four different nine-patch blocks, perhaps 18″ square (116.1 sq cm) or more. Some of the patches would be pieced and others left plain so that it would not be nearly so much work as "Trip Around the World." The pattern could be adapted for use as a medallion or a whole quilt of any size from crib to king.

The next month I was still working with "Nine-patch." You would think that by then I would have grown tired of it, but it still entices my attention like a favorite melody. This time, for Pattern 55, the center patch of a larger nine-patch was divided into a small one. This was surrounded by a border of small squares. I drew several rows of nine-patch blocks just like this. In alternate blocks I made matching nine-patches in the corners also and produced "Double Nine-patch." The change from that to a "Double Irish Chain" block was almost compulsive.

As I continued to shade in all the blocks to match, a few ideas for adding to the little center design came to me so I experimented with them at the bottom of the page.

These are the ways that I explore possible patterns and designs and variations. It is almost as though the designs are there all the time helping me to make them appear on paper. Was it Michelangelo who said that he did not create the figures which he sculpted from marble, but that they were there all along waiting for him to free them?

It is my belief that the ability to be creative in one or often many ways is the gift of every person. No one person can find these ways for another nor can anyone tell another "the way" to develop such abilities. Each individual must find personal ways of doing this. A few general principles however might apply to all at least to some extent. I think that an attitude of pleasurable anticipation always helps. It is important to recognize even a small idea and to encourage it by following its leading. Even if it does not appear to have promise, give it a chance. If it does not work, remember that we learn as much from our mistakes as from our successes—maybe

57

Illus. 52, Pattern 54. "Variation on a Square."

more. Do not throw away, at once, sketches that seem to be unsuccessful. Much later when rediscovered they may develop into something very pleasing. Don't force yourself to continue to try to make drawings when it has ceased to be a pleasure. This is the most certain way I know to cut off the flow of ideas. Wait for another time when you can enter into the activity eagerly expecting something to happen and to enjoy being a part of it.

Finally, do not be too quick to decide that all this is not for you. Give yourself the chance to make that most wonderful discovery of all, that wishing—and really believing in yourself—*can* make it so.

Illus. 53, Pattern 55. "Irish Chain Around the World."

4

New Approaches

The traditional method for marking pieces on fabric is to make a template and mark one piece at a time, fitting the pieces as closely together as possible. Pieces marked for hand sewing are usually marked without seam allowances and a space for them is left between the marked shapes. Sometimes both the finished shape and the added seam allowances are marked. Pieces marked for machine stitching are marked with seam allowances added. In all cases they are marked on the wrong side of the fabric unless there is a special reason not to do so, such as centering a print design on the piece.

There is always a tendency for pieces marked by this method to get out of line gradually no matter how carefully it is done. For this reason the methods described in this chapter for marking pieces are better as well as faster, even if only a single layer of pieces is to be cut. If several layers are to be cut at once, considerably more time can be saved and accurate pieces produced if the scissors are very sharp and sufficient pins are used. (This does not always hold true for soft fabrics of blended fibres but it does for 100% cottons and firmer blends.)

Most of the marking and cutting methods presented can benefit either the hand sewer or those who piece by machine. Those who prefer to have the finished sizes of shapes marked rather than those which include seam allowances will find special instructions and diagrams for adapting the marking methods for those needs on pages 62–64.

When I first saw the work of the Seminole Indians, I was immediately interested in the sewing methods which could produce such tiny designs. As I began to try them for larger patterns, however, I found that they were not always as practical at that scale as some methods I had been using. Some of the Seminole methods I did find helpful and others I modified to fit my needs. Some of these I mentioned in Chapter 2, as I described the methods used for Seminole piecing. Some of it may be repeated here in connection with instructions for stitching patterns of larger pieces. Other parts of the information which was described in greater detail at that time will only be referred to here, by name perhaps, at the appropriate places.

The methods I use are actually composites of all those I have learned or taught myself to use in sewing. They provide me with an assortment of ways of handling various sewing situations. From these I can select the one which seems best to fit the needs of the occasion. There are some basic procedures I employ as a matter of course, always reserving the privilege of substituting others. These basic methods I will discuss first.

To begin at the beginning, I draw on graph paper a diagram of the quilt just as I plan to make it. I let one square on the paper represent one unit of measurement in the quilt pattern. If necessary, I tape two or more sheets of paper together to include the entire top in the diagram if it cannot be scaled down to fit one sheet. I draw every block in place,

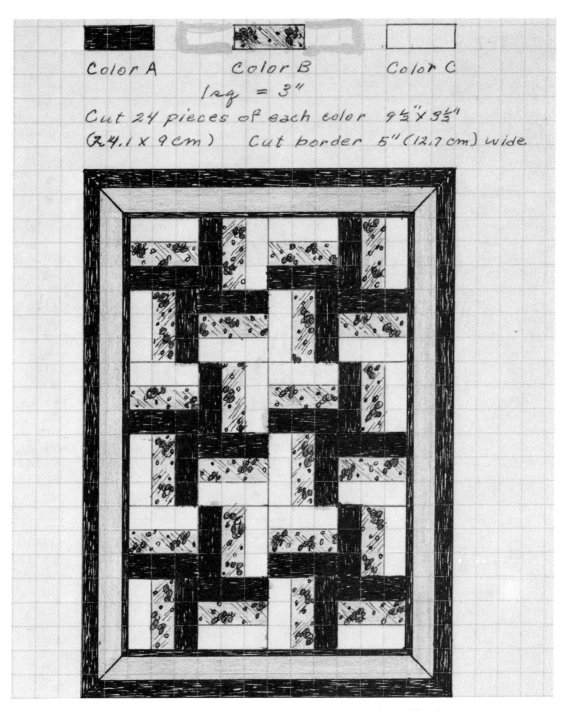

Color A   Color B   Color C

1 sq = 3"

Cut 24 pieces of each color 9½" x 3½"
(24.1 x 9 cm)   Cut border 5" (12.7 cm) wide

Illus. 54, Pattern 56. "Windmill" (46" × 63" or 116.8 × 160cm).

set with lattice or setting blocks or whatever I plan to use in piecing the top. I draw in all the pieces on at least one block—but usually on all of them. Then I shade or color in the pieces to get an idea of the general effect this will give (Illus. 54).

This diagram is my guide for all the information I need for piecing. It tells me the overall measurements of the top. It shows the size and number of the blocks and/or other parts of the top. It is also a guide for all the piecing methods that must be done.

I can use the diagram to help me in figuring the amount of fabric I will need because it shows the number of pieces required and the size of each different shape, all of which are included in the drawing.

When the quilt is finished it is handy to file the diagram away, together with the amounts of fabric used and any other information of interest for future reference.

All washable fabric which comes into my home goes first to the laundry before it goes to the sewing room. It is then ready for use at any time I want it. I may postpone the ironing, which would likely have to be done over anyway. Fabrics, which are removed from the drier without long waiting, are not often badly wrinkled anyway. The exceptions are long pieces of fabric which become twisted while tumbling.

After the fabric is laundered and I am ready to use it, I lay it out on the cutting board. If I am going to cut numbers of pieces with straight sides I almost always mark them directly on the wrong side of the fabric, using a metal or plastic rule (a yardstick will do if it is absolutely straight on the edge and if the markings are truly accurate—not all are!). Pieces such as squares, rectangles, triangles, diamonds, rhomboids, etc., are marked in this way. For some straight-sided shapes I use a template to do part of the marking. I also use a template for marking octagons and hexagons as well as pieces with one or more curved sides.

To mark squares or rectangles I begin by straightening the end of the fabric (Illus. 55). I lay the selvages together along a lengthwise line on the cutting board. Then I place my rule near the end of the fabric and along a crossways line. Then I draw a line with a fairly soft lead pencil. This is much faster than pulling a thread, which likely will not work if the fabric has been treated in some way (such as for permanent press) or if it is woven of blended fibres.

It may not be possible to straighten even 100% cotton if it has been treated and if, when the fabric comes through the laundry, the crossways threads are still warped out of straight. Woven plaids, checks and crossways stripes which are warped must have the measurement of the pieces marked along the warped threads and cut that way. This produces warped pieces, but they will be pulled into place by the unwarped pieces around them and held in place by quilting.

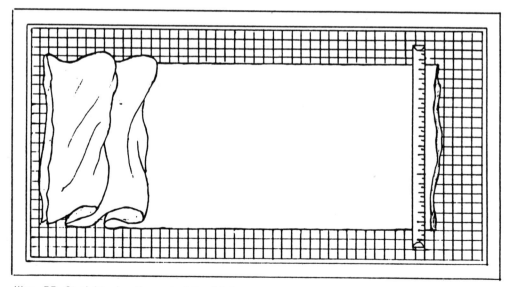

Illus. 55. Straightening the end of the fabric.

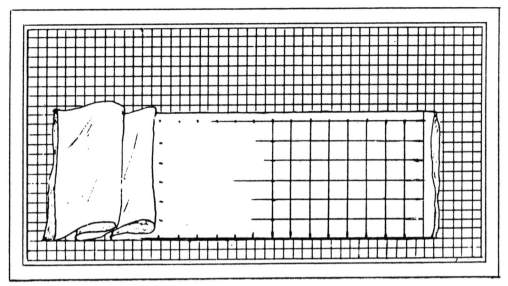

Illus. 56. Marking pieces on the fabric.

If you have only untreated cottons and they can be ironed to lie straight with the lengthwise and cross grain when a thread is pulled, so much the better. If not, use the other method.

After straightening the end, measure and draw a line ¼″ (.6cm) from the selvage edge. From this line measure repeats of the width of the piece along the first line drawn to straighten the end (Illus. 56). Near the other end of the fabric, or about every 24″ (61.0cm) along it, lay the yardstick along another crossways line on the board, but do not draw a line. Begin at the line along the selvage to mark repeats of the *width* of the piece as before. Draw lines parallel to the selvages which join these marks.

Even if I intend to sew long strips of fabric, which will later be cut into pieces, I *mark* these pieces on the fabric before I cut the strips. To do this I begin at the first line drawn to straighten the fabric and from there I measure, along the line at the selvage, repeats of the length of the piece. I repeat this process along the lengthwise line nearest the fold of the fabric. These marks are joined with crossways lines on the fabric.

If I need squares or rectangles of the same size to be cut of two different fabrics and these pieces are to be sewn together in pairs in the process of piecing, then I mark a single layer of fabric (usually the lighter of the two) and lay the two fabrics right sides together. I pin every 6″–8″ (15.2–20.3cm) along the

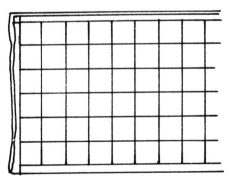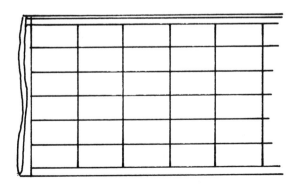

Illus. 57. Marking squares and rectangles.

63

lengthwise or crossways line (depending upon which side of the piece is to be joined). Then I stitch ¼″ (.6cm) from that line on *both* sides. I do this along *every other line* drawn for these pieces, sewing *before* I do any cutting. If very long pieces of fabric are to be sewn in this way, I usually cut them into sections along crossways lines for easier handling. This is much faster than matching the edges of long strips for stitching and then marking the strips into pieces after sewing.

After I have sewn my strips, I cut the strips and press the seam allowances in one direction. Then I lay the two fabrics back right sides together again and hold them firmly or pin them together and cut along the crossways lines where the other measurement for the pieces has already been marked.

If several different fabrics are to be cut into pieces of the same size, I fold one fabric in half lengthwise, wrong-side-out, and mark it as described. Then I fold each additional fabric (up to three more) in the same way and add them one by one under the marked fabric. I make sure all the selvages are lying together, and pin them with each addition.

I lay out all the layers smoothly on the cutting board and pin the marked pieces near the corners and through all layers. If the pieces are large I also pin along the sides of the pieces, using enough pins to keep the layers from shifting. It is essential to have very sharp, good-quality scissors to cut this many layers. My 8″ (20.3cm) Ginghers cut them with ease. If your scissors cannot do this, use fewer layers.

I cut away the selvages first. Next I cut off the strip along the fold and save it for string piecing. After that I trim away the irregular piece (if any) at the end and cut crossways strips of pieces, and finally cut the strips into pieces. My clock tells me that it is faster to mark and cut a stack of six to eight pieces, which I then chain-sew, than it is to mark long strips of fabric, even in layers which must be marked into pieces or segments after they are sewn together.

If I want to cut half-square triangles, I first make a paper pattern by drawing a square the size (without seam allowances) that I want the

pieced triangles to form. It is necessary for the corners of your squares to be absolutely square (90°). For this reason, I recommend using plastic triangles, which can be purchased in any art supply shop. For a half-square triangle I fold the square in half diagonally and cut along the fold (Illus. 58). To the resulting triangle I add ¼″ (.6cm) seam al-

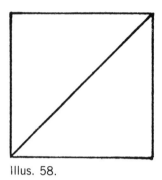

Illus. 58.

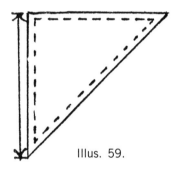

Illus. 59.

lowances all around (Illus. 59). I then measure one of the sides which had been a side of the square (not the diagonal side) and that is the measurement I use to draw squares on the fabric. After the squares are drawn I then use my yardstick to draw diagonal lines in one direction from corner to corner of the squares (Illus. 60).

If the triangles are to be sewn to other triangles of the same size along the diagonal sides, I mark a single layer of fabric and add the other fabric right sides together under it just as was described for pairs of squares or rectangles (Illus. 61). I pin the diagonal lines near the corners and stitch ¼″ (.6cm) from the line on both sides. I am careful not to stitch across the corners of other pieces between the ends of the diagonal stitching.

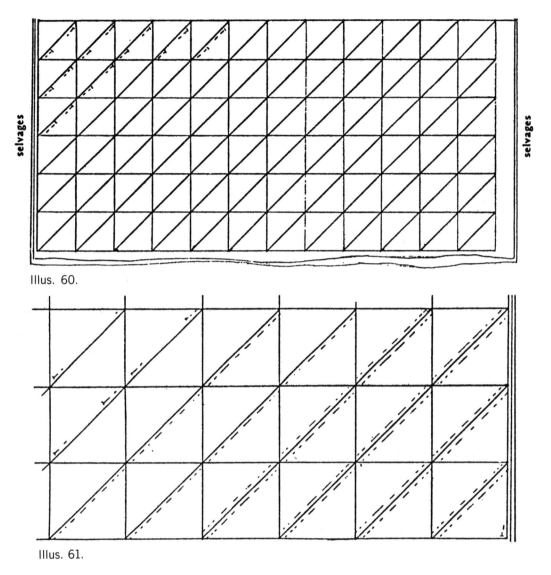

Illus. 60.

Illus. 61.

Then I cut along all the marked lines. The triangles have now all been pieced into squares and it was much easier to stitch the bias seams before they were cut.

To check the accuracy of my stitching, as I press the seam allowances, I draw on laundered muslin a square of the same size I cut as a pattern in the beginning. This time I add the seam allowances to all sides of the square. The piece of muslin used must be large enough to allow room for ironing without hitting the pins I use to fasten it to the ironing board. This muslin pattern I call an ironing template (Illus. 62). I press the pieced half-squares over this drawn square to check their

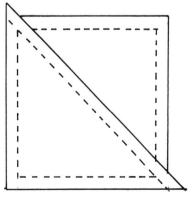

Illus. 62.

size. If they are too large I know I did not sew my seam quite wide enough. If the squares are too small the seam was too wide. If there is a mistake, it is more convenient to know it at this point in the piecing when it is easy to make adjustments as needed, than it is to find out later when the pieced squares do not fit the other pieces of the pattern.

For quarter-square triangles the procedure is much the same. I begin with the paper square of the size I want after the triangles are pieced—without seam allowances (Illus.

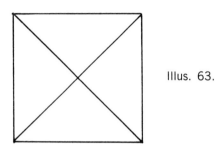

Illus. 63.

63). I fold it *both* ways diagonally and cut out one of the triangles. To this I add ¼″ (.6cm) seam allowances all around and measure the side which was one side of the square (Illus. 64). This gives the measurement of the square I need to mark on the fabric.

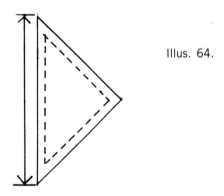

Illus. 64.

After this is done I draw diagonal lines in *both* directions across the marked squares and pin this fabric right sides together to the fabric for the triangles I want to sew to the ones I have marked. I sew these triangles in exactly the same way that I did the half-squares—along one diagonal line only and ¼″ (.6cm) from it on both sides of it.

I cut the triangles exactly as before—along the lines for the squares and along only the diagonal lines where stitching was done. This again gives me squares, which I press in the same way as before to check the accuracy of the size.

One triangle of the squares just stitched is marked from the corner to the middle of the stitched diagonal seam. Using a small ruler as a guide, I extend this line to the opposite corner of the other triangle on *half* the squares stitched. Then I pin two squares right sides together so that each triangle lies on a triangle of the different fabric. The seams must be carefully matched where the diagonal line is drawn across them. The seam allowances are already pressed so that they lie in opposite directions. I also pin the corners at the ends of the diagonal line.

Again I sew ¼″ (.6cm) from the line on both sides, stitching this bias seam also before it is cut. I cut along the line between the stitching and then press these new pieced squares over the ironing template to check for sewing accuracy.

Half-Rectangles

A rectangle is a plain figure with four right (90°) angles and opposite sides of equal length. (Thus a square is actually a special kind of rectangle!) Half-rectangle patterns can be made in the same way as half-squares. Add seam allowances to the measurements for the finished half-rectangle. Then measure the length and the width of the shape and use these measurements to mark rectangular pieces on the fabric. Draw diagonal lines from corner to corner in one direction only (as is done for half-squares) to divide the rectangles in half as in Illus. 65. (See "Two Pinwheels," Pattern 89 in Chapter 6, for a design which uses half-rectangles.)

Isosceles Triangles and Equilateral Triangles

An isosceles triangle is one which has two equal angles and therefore has two equal sides. If all angles and all sides are the same it

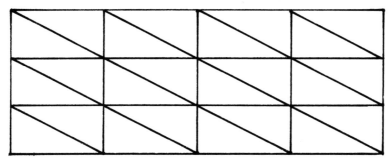

Illus. 65. Marking half-rectangles.

is an equilateral triangle. A 60° diamond can be folded across in half at the corners to make an equilateral triangle. Other half-diamonds are isosceles triangles. A half-square is also an isosceles triangle, but its 90° angle makes it easier to cut by dividing a square. For other isosceles triangles (including equilateral triangles) a slightly different method is required for marking the fabric into pieces.

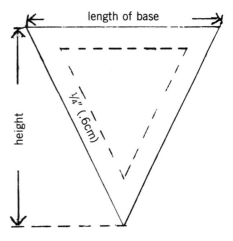

Illus. 67. Seam allowances added, mark this size triangle on the fabric.

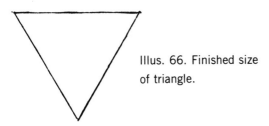

Illus. 66. Finished size of triangle.

Draw the finished shape required (Illus. 66) and add seam allowances. Measure the height and the base as shown in Illus. 67. Mark strips across the fabric, using the measurement of the height of the triangle. Begin at the fold of the fabric (if it is to be folded) or at one edge with selvage marked off. Mark spaces along the first line at the end of the fabric and also along the third or fifth or any other odd-numbered line, as needed, according to the number of strips to be marked. Join the marks diagonally in both directions as shown (Illus. 68) to form the triangles. Illus. 69 is a quilt block called "Tippecanoe" (Pattern 57) which was the nickname of General William Henry Harrison after his victory in the battle of that name. He later became our ninth president (1840).

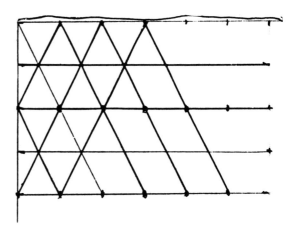

Illus. 68. Marking the fabric for isosceles triangles.

To draft the pattern, draw or cut a square the size you need using the unit measurements given and draw or fold lines to divide it into four equal squares. Mark a point halfway along each dividing line. From these points draw or fold the three lines which divide the square into four triangles. The middle triangle is an isosceles triangle. On each side of it is a half-rectangle and at the base is a half-square. Four squares form the block.

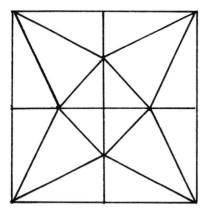

Illus. 69, Pattern 57. "Tippecanoe."

Illus. 70. Folding a 45° diamond.

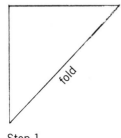

Step 1

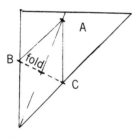

Step 4

Drafting 45° Diamonds
(Makes an eight-point star)

Method I. Diamonds can be easily drawn or folded with paper (Illus. 70). Cut or draw a half-square that is larger than the finished length of the diamond you want (Step 1). Fold it once (or mark a line) as shown (Step 2). Measure the length of the diamond along the fold or line and make a mark there. Bring the point of the triangle to mark and crease the fold (or make a mark halfway along this line and draw another line perpendicular to it at that point). Draw lines *AB* and *AC* where the crease (or line) meets the sides of the triangle. This forms the diamond. Add seam allowances before marking the fabric.

Method II. You may prefer to draft the diamond with a protractor. (See Illus. 71.) If so, draw a line on paper the length of the finished diamond. Label one end of the line *A* and the other *B*. First place your protractor so that the center point is at *A* and the mark for 90° lies along the line. If your diamond is small it may be necessary to lengthen the line to reach the 90° mark. With the protractor in this position mark point *C* at 112½° and point *D* at 67½°. Draw lines *AC* and *AD*. Next place the center point of the protractor at *B* with the 90° mark on line *AB*. Mark point *E* at 67½° and point *F* at 112½°. Draw lines *BE* and *BF* to complete the diamond.

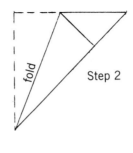

Step 2

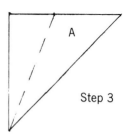

Step 3

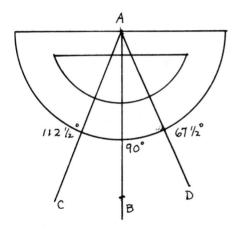

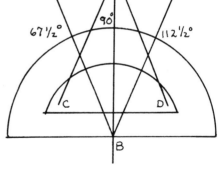

Illus. 71. Drafting a 45° diamond with a protractor.

Drafting 60° Diamonds
(Makes a six-point star)

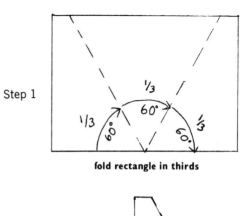

fold rectangle in thirds

Method I. To draft a 60° diamond on paper, mark or crease a point halfway along one side (Step 1, Illus. 72) and make two lines or folds which divide the paper into three equal angles. Working with one of the three parts (Step 2), fold or draw a line which divides the angle in half (Step 3). Mark the length of the diamond on the fold or line (Step 4). Fold the points of the paper to the mark (Step 5), or make a mark halfway between the point and the mark and draw a second line perpendicular to the first. Draw lines AB and AC to complete the diamond (Step 6).

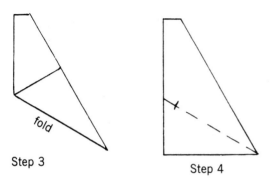

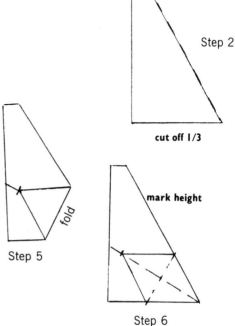

Illus. 72. Folding a 60° diamond.

Method II. To draft a 60° diamond with a protractor (see Illus. 73), draw on paper a line which is the finished length of the diamond. Mark point *A* at one end and *B* at the other. Begin by placing the center point of the protractor at *A* so that the 90° mark falls on line *AB*. This line can be extended if necessary. With the protractor in this position, mark point *C* at 120° and *D* at 60°. Draw lines *AC* and *AD*.

Repeat the process with the center point of the protractor at *B*. Mark *E* at 60° and *F* at 120°. Draw lines *BE* and *BF*. This completes the diamond shape.

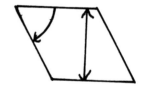

Illus. 74.

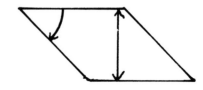

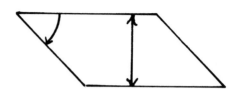

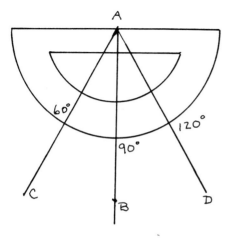

Illus. 73. Drafting a 60° diamond with a protractor.

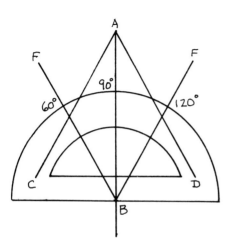

Marking Diamonds on Fabric

Add seam allowances to the diamond shape and mark strips on the fabric the width of the diamond at the arrows. (See Illus. 74). If the fabric is folded, the bottom diamonds will be the reverse of the top ones. On solid color fabric or most prints this will make no difference except for which side of the diamond will be on the grain and which will be bias. This could make a difference in the stitching of the pieces and also in the direction of the grainline of the diamond in relation to that of other pieces of the pattern (a situation to be considered if you are trying to keep all grainlines consistent on the top). If any of these exceptions is important to your project, mark a single layer of fabric. Additional layers must have the same side up. If none of the above mentioned exceptions is important to your project, you can fold the fabric lengthwise and/or crossways to make more layers.

You have three choices for marking diamonds on the fabric.

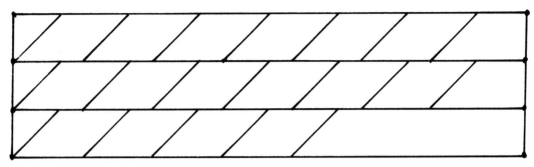

Illus. 75. Method 1.

Method 1. You can mark strips across the fabric the width of the diamond (see Illus. 75). Then make a template of the diamond and lay it along the strips to mark the diagonal ends of the figure.

Method 2. You can mark the diamonds directly on the fabric using measurements (Illus 76). First mark strips across the fabric the width of the diamond as shown in Illus.

74 (be sure to add seam allowance). Then measure the length of one side of diamond to mark repeats of that length along the first line. For 45° diamonds, mark repeats of that length again along every third line as needed. For 60° diamonds, the additional lines marked with repeats must be marked on every odd-numbered line from left to right. In either case, join the marks diagonally to complete the diamonds.

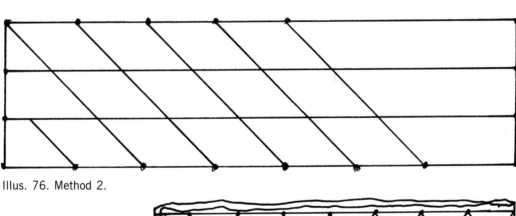

Illus. 76. Method 2.

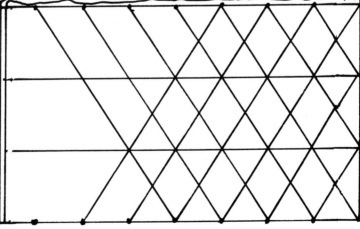

Illus. 77. Method 3.

Method 3. Sometimes it is desirable to have diamonds cut on the lengthwise grain (Illus. 77). In this case, draft the diamond of the angle and length desired and add seam allowances. Measure the length of the diamond from point to point and the width from corner to corner. Mark strips across the fabric as wide as the length of the diamond. Then beginning at the fold on the first line marked near the end of the fabric, mark spaces that are the width of the diamond. Repeat this on any other line as needed. Draw diagonal lines in both directions from mark to mark to form the diamonds. Diamonds cut on the lengthwise grain of the fabric do not reverse if the fabric is folded in either direction.

Rhomboids. A rhomboid is similar to a diamond but different because two opposite sides are longer than the others. If your quilt pattern includes a rhomboid among the pieces, make a template of the piece, including seam allowances, and mark it on the fabric in the same way as for diamonds by Method 1, or you can mark rhomboids directly on the fabric by Method 2.

Drafting an Octagon and an Eight-point Star in a Square

Illus. 78 shows two methods for drafting an eight-point star. The lines on the square can either be drawn or folded. In Version A, all points of the star touch the corners of the octagon. Begin by drawing all the dashed lines in the square in the order of the numbers. Each line divides the space between two other lines in half and each line passes through the center point. Next draw all the solid lines connecting ends of the dashed lines as shown. These form the octagon and the star. Cut out or measure the diamond and add seam allowances to get the correct size.

Sometimes it is desirable to have the points center on each side of the octagon instead of each corner of it. If this is the case, draw all the dashed lines as before. The octagon is formed by the sides of the square and the diagonal lines drawn at the corners as in A. Draw the star by drawing lines from between the ends of a different set of dashed lines as seen in B. This star is a little smaller than the other.

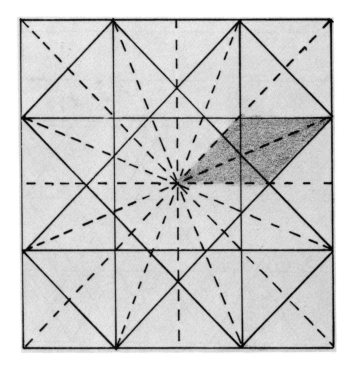

Illus. 78A. Folding paper to draft octagons with eight-point stars.

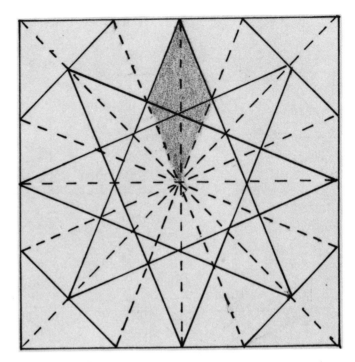

Illus. 78B.

Piecing an Eight-point Star in a Square

An eight-point star in a square is a block called "Lemoine Star" (Illus. 79, Pattern 58). This pattern calls for squares to be set between two diamonds to form a corner star.

Begin by sewing a diamond to a square. The seam should stop at the point where it meets the stitching line of the next seam (Step 1). Backstitch or tie the threads or let the last few stitches be 20 to the inch (these will not work out).

Sew another diamond to the adjoining side of the square as shown in Step 2, ending the seam in the same way as before.

Now fold the square on the diagonal so that the two diamonds lie exactly one on the other and sew the two together as shown in Step 3, ending the seam as before.

Sew four of these groups of three pieces (Step 4) and press them.

Then use the same method to stitch two groups to a triangle to make two halves of the block (Step 5) and to set the two halves together with triangles at the sides (Step 6). This leaves a seam unstitched across the middle.

Fold the block as shown in Step 7 and pin the center points together carefully. Then stitch from each side to the center without sewing over any seam allowances of other diamonds. Press the seam allowances of the diamonds so that they all turn in one direction.

If you prefer not to set in squares by either method, you can cut the squares and triangles and piece half of each to a diamond and then piece the block. Be sure that when you sew the half-blocks together, however, that you sew from the edges just to the center as directed and press the same way.

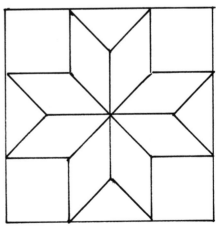

"Lemoine Star"

73

Illus. 79. Piecing an eight-point star (Pattern 58. "Lemoine Star").

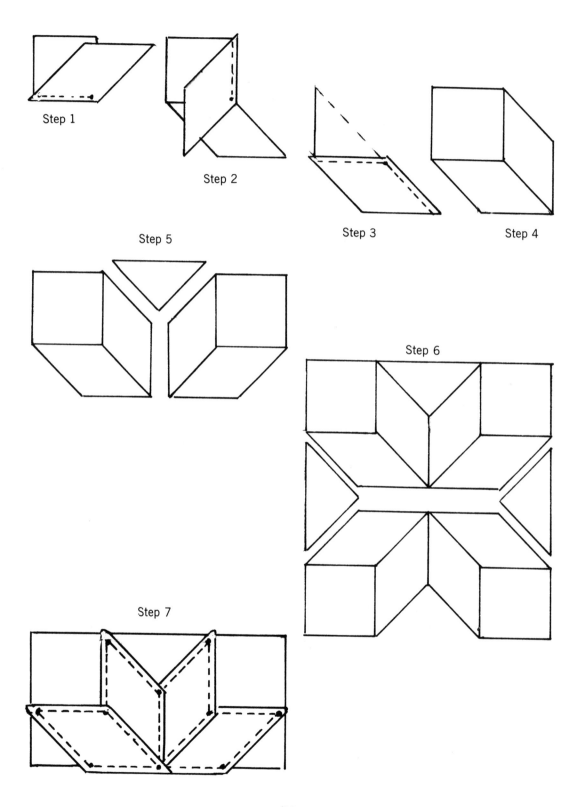

Step 1

Step 2

Step 3

Step 4

Step 5

Step 6

Step 7

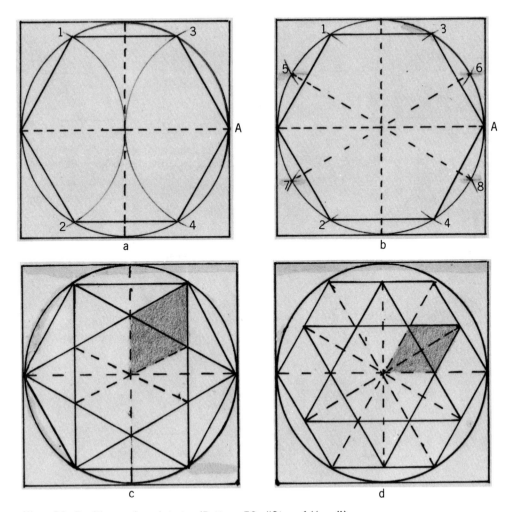

Illus. 80. Drafting a six-point star (Pattern 59. "Star of Hope").

Drafting a Hexagon and a Six-point Star in a Circle and a Square

Draw a circle with a diameter the same as the widest measurement of the hexagon you want. Draw a square which fits the outside of the circle. The length of the sides will be the same as the diameter of the circle. Fold or draw the dashed lines which cross at the center of the circle from the middle of the sides.

With the compass set at the same radius as for the circle, place the point at each end of line A and draw the two arcs which cross the circle at points 1, 2, 3 and 4. The hexagon is formed within the circle by drawing lines from point to point around the circle where these curved and dashed lines cross it or

touch it. All this is shown in Part a of Illus. 80. The star is formed by drawing lines from corner to corner of the hexagon in the manner shown in Part b.

If you wish the points of your star to touch the sides of the hexagon instead of the corners, this also can be done. Construct the hexagon in the circle as before. Next set the radius of the compass as it was for marking points 1, 2, 3 and 4. Place the point of the compass at each end of Line B and make points 5, 6, 7 and 8 on the circle, and connect opposite points with lines as shown in Part c. Use the points where these lines and Line B cross the sides of the hexagon to construct the star as in Part d.

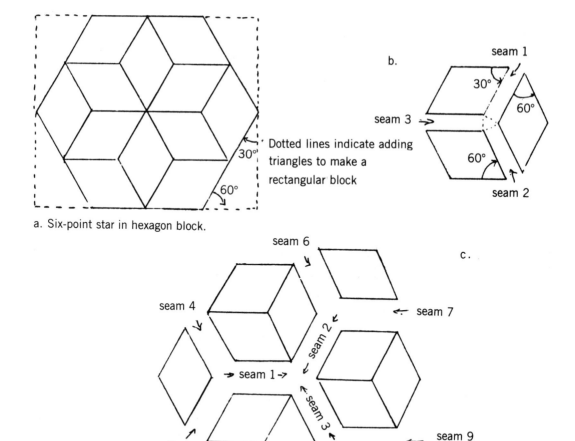

a. Six-point star in hexagon block.

Dotted lines indicate adding triangles to make a rectangular block

b.

Illus. 81. Piecing a hexagon with a six-point star (Pattern 60).

Piecing a Six-point Star in a Hexagon

Illus. 81 shows the piecing of a six-point star made of diamonds. It is a variation of "Lemoine Star" (Pattern 59). The diamonds between the points of the star are the same size as those used to piece the star. Remember that no seam should be stitched beyond the point when that seam meets another stitching line.

Setting in a Square

Sometimes it is desirable to set in a square. Pattern 61 in Illus. 82, was designed especially to do this. The method can be used for any other pattern as well if there is a square in the center and other pieces must be added around it. The trick is to piece first everything that goes around the square and then set the square into the space left for it.

Illus. 82. Setting in a square (Pattern 61).

Step 1

Step 2

Step 4

Step 3

Step 5   Step 6

Illus. 82 shows first the piecing of the border which goes around the square. It is made up of segments of a three-strip set pieced as a border. In this case four segments are pieced as shown. A square is removed from the end of one segment. It can then be added to the side of that segment if the light colored pieces are the same color. If they are not, then a square which matches the outside pieces must be used (Step 1). Step 2 shows this piecing complete. Make four units in the same way and join them into a square border as shown in Step 3.

Measure the stitching line for the square opening and mark a square of fabric that size using a water-soluble marker. If this will not show on your fabric, then mark the square with basting stitches. Add ½" (1.3cm) seam allowances all around for easier handling.

Staystitch just inside the stitching line of the square opening. Snip the fabric to the stitched corners and press the seam allowances under. Then lay the pieced border over the prepared square, matching the turned-under edge of the border to the marked or basted stitching line of the square. Pin the border in place, catching only the seam allowances with the pins. Fold one side back and stitch the seam as shown in Step 4. Stitch across the seam allowance of the square exactly to the first dot, then straight across both layers to the second dot and on across the seam allowance of the square only. Repeat this stitching for each side of the square.

Step 5 shows just one of several ways of mitring a border. Sew the border pieces the exact length of the stitching line as indicated by the dots. Be sure not to sew beyond this point. Then fold the piece on the diagonal so that two border strips lie exactly together (Step 6). Lay a long rule precisely along the diagonal fold so that it continues across the border. Mark this diagonal on the border and stitch as shown. Sew only as far as the dot, not across the seam allowances. Unfold the piece and check to be sure the mitre is true before trimming away the extra fabric at the ends of the border strips.

Piecing a Curved Seam

Curved seams are considered a challenge. With just a little practice (some do it perfectly the first time) they can be pieced by machine, perhaps more easily than by hand. When marking the pieces, be sure to mark the middle of both curves so that they can be matched correctly.

Pin the pieces together about ⅜" (1.0cm) from the beginning and the end of the seam and at the marked middle of the curved edges (Illus. 83, Step 1). I like to stitch with the quarter circle (convex) piece on top, but some prefer to have the other piece up. Do not snip the seam allowance of either curve. The bias areas will ease as needed during the stitching so that the pieces will fit together. Do not use more than the three pins indicated, for extra ones will interfere with the easing process of both layers.

Relax and sew slowly using both hands to guide the pieces and ease them together as

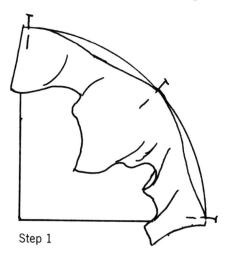

Step 1

Illus. 83. Piecing a curved seam (Pattern 62. "Wonder of the World").

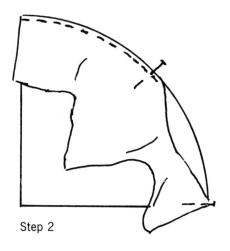

Step 2

Illus. 83 A
"Wonder of the World"

you stitch (Step 2). Stop and remove the pins at the last possible stitch or "tiptoe" over them as you turn the wheel by hand. Do not hurry the learning process. More speed will come as your skill develops.

The blocks shown in the diagram are a "Drunkard's Path" variation called "Wonder of the World" (Pattern 62).

Setting in a Circle

I have never seen or read any instructions for doing this and have been told by several people that circles and rings must be appliquéd by hand. It is true that a small circle in the middle of a large piece is awkward to piece into place. A larger circle such as is shown in Pattern 63 (Illus. 84) is, however, perhaps even easier to handle than setting in a square or piecing a curved seam. The important thing is that both the circle and the round hole to which it is pieced *must be* accurately marked and stitched. This is true of all piecing, of course, so you should be accustomed to it.

Make a template of the circle for the hole. Use this to mark the hole in the fabric which will surround your circle. Use it also to mark the stitching line of the circle. Use a water-soluble marking pen or straight pins which are then replaced by basting stitches. If your inner circle is of unpieced fabric do not cut the circle out but only mark it on the fabric. If your inner circle is pieced to form that shape (a circle) that is all right.

Staystitch the circular hole and snip the seam allowance about every ⅓″–½″ (.9–1.3cm). Turn the seam allowance under and press. Then fit the round opening over the circle carefully matching the opening to the marked or basted line on the inner circle. Pin all around the circle, catching only the seam allowances together as in b. If you are a beginner and feel uneasy about doing this piecing you can pin the pieces over (and to) a piece of paper or tear-away interfacing (indicated by the dashed lines) to stabilize the work in progress.

The design used for this demonstration is one I call "Circle of Hope," a variant of "Star of Hope," Pattern 59.

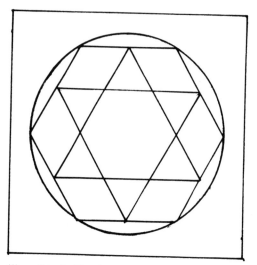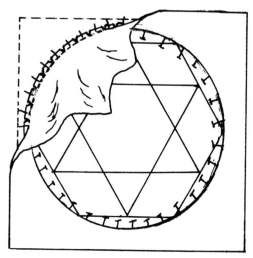

Illus. 84. Setting in a circle (Pattern 63, "Circle of Hope," variant of "Star of Hope," Pattern 59).

Piecing Hexagons

"Grandmother's Flower Garden" (Pattern 64) always has been a favorite pattern. It is faster and easier to piece by machine than by hand and accuracy is not sacrificed in the process. This is true even if the hexagons are only 1" (2.5cm). The method may seem a little strange and backward as it is described, but the important thing is that it works.

First piece the ring of hexagons which surrounds the center hexagon (Step 1). Stitch only from seam allowance to seam allowance as indicated by the dots. Then set the center hexagon into the ring in much the same way that squares are set in (see Illus. 82). Pin and stitch the seams one at a time (Step 2). Stitch only between the dots, from seam allowance to seam allowance, *never* beyond the dot into the seam allowance (Step 2). Backstitch or tie threads.

Continue to piece any additional ring(s) to be added to the previous one by the same process, one seam at a time stitched from seam allowance to seam allowance.

Other hexagon patterns are pieced in this manner.

Marking the Fabric with Pieces of the Finished Size

Most hand piecers and some who piece by machine prefer to mark the finished size of the piece on the fabric, leaving space for seam allowances between. This method assures that they can sew exactly on the stitching line. No matter how carefully the template is placed on the fabric, however, the pieces tend to drift a little out of line causing some possible deviation from the grainline and some slight loss of fabric when adjustments are made. Some who mark this way like to mark seam allowances around the pieces as well. This sometimes means the extra expense of templates made for this purpose or the making of extra templates.

Whichever way the marking is done, it is necessary that each layer of the fabric be marked separately. The following suggestions are included for those who prefer this type of marking. It eliminates much of the use of templates and the cutting will go faster as well.

If you have not already done so, read first the instructions given for marking the various

80

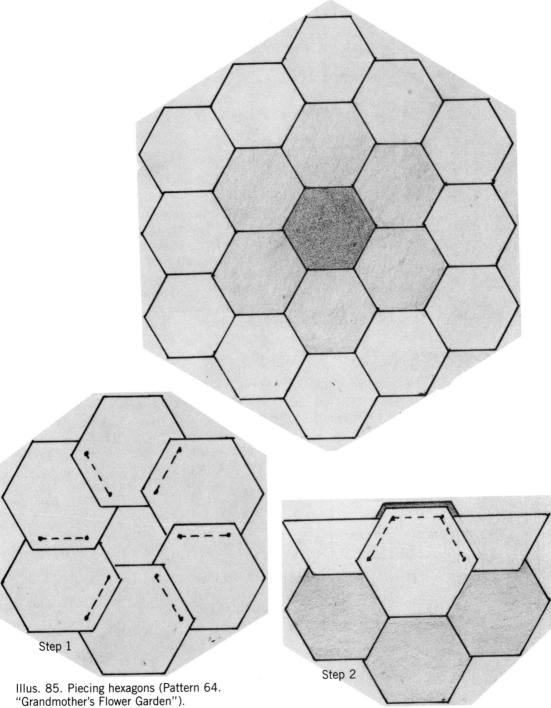

Illus. 85. Piecing hexagons (Pattern 64. "Grandmother's Flower Garden").

pieces on the fabric so that you will be thoroughly familiar with the general methods. The instructions here are intended as supplements to those and will not necessarily be completely understandable without them.

For squares, rectangles, and diamond shapes no templates are required (Illus. 86 and 87). These pieces can be marked directly on the fabric. If you wish, the individual seam allowances can also be marked in the

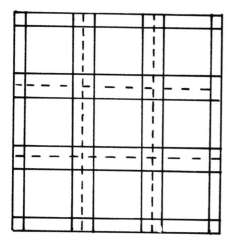

Illus. 86. 1" (2.5cm) square.

same process instead of just the space of two seam allowances between the pieces. (See dashed lines.)

Begin marking squares or rectangles by drawing the line to straighten the end of the fabric (if this is needed). Then draw the line ¼" (.6cm) from the edge to cut away the selvage. Do this just along one edge unless the pieces come right to the other selvage.

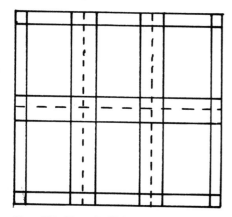

Illus. 87. 1" × 2" (2.5 × 5.1cm) rectangle.

Along the straight end of the fabric (or the line drawn there), begin at the selvage line to mark spaces. The first space will be ¼" (.6cm) from the line marked at the selvage. This is for one seam allowance. Then mark the measurement of the width of the square or rectangle. The next mark will be ½" (1.3cm) fur-

ther along for two seam allowances between the pieces. (If you want to mark the cutting line also, make two ¼" or .6cm spaces instead of the ½" or 1.3cm space.) Continue to mark measurements of pieces alternately with seam allowances along the line, finishing with one ¼" (.6cm) seam allowance as shown. Repeat this same marking across the fabric as described in the general instructions, about every 24" (61cm) or less. Join the marks with lines parallel to the selvage.

Along the selvage line mark first the ¼" (.6cm) seam allowance for the first row of pieces. Then mark the length of the square or rectangle, followed by the ½" (1.3cm) seam allowance (or two ¼" ones). Continue marking these two measurements alternately, as needed, ending with a ¼" (.6cm) seam allowance. Repeat this set of markings two or more times on vertical lines already drawn on the fabric. Join these marks to complete the marking of the pieces.

The marking of diamonds and other similar shapes is done in much the same way (Illus. 88). First mark the horizontal lines on the fabric beginning with a ¼" (.6cm) space for the first seam allowance. Then measure the figure as indicated in Illus. 89 to find the width of the piece and use that measurement alternately with ½" (1.3cm) for two seam allowances (except for the final single seam allowance of ¼" (.6cm).

A study of Illus. 90 will make clear the way these diagonal widths are measured. Notice that the seam allowance is ¼" (.6cm) from the stitching line. When it is measured for marking on the fabric, however, the horizontal distance between the two lines must be measured and used because the spaces will be marked along horizontal lines on the fabric. For a 45° diamond or rhomboid the horizontal width of one seam allowance is ⅜" (1.0cm), ¾" (1.9cm) for two. The horizontal width of the seam allowance of a line drawn at a 30° angle to the horizontal line is ⅝" (1.6cm) for one, 1¼" (3.2cm) for two. Mark the measurements which apply to your shape of diamond or rhomboid for seam allowances drawn on the fabric alternately with the measurements for the finished piece.

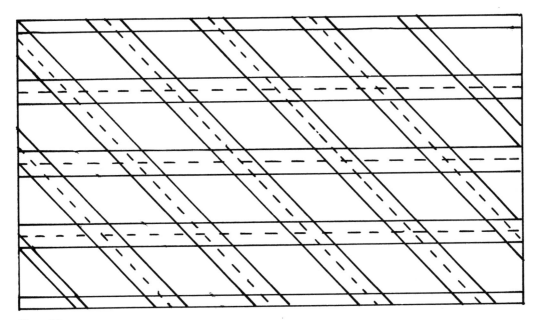

Illus. 88.

These are the basic shapes which are used in the construction of the patterns in this book.

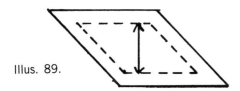

Illus. 89.

The next basic method I use is chain-sewing. As an example we will use Pattern 53 (Illus. 51) from Chapter 3. This pattern is made up of small squares which are arranged to form a design. The squares would be cut eight layers at a time as described.

The diagram (Illus. 91) shown is for one block, which could make a pillow top (if the unit measure equalled 1½", or 3.8cm, plus seam allowance) or a baby quilt (if the unit measure equals 3" or 7.6cm) with borders added. Enough blocks could be set solid to make a full quilt of any size. The piecing method would be the same in any case.

On this diagram the rows are numbered across to make clear my instructions. If you have trouble keeping your place on a larger diagram of more rows, use a bobby pin to slip along the page as a marker.

In piecing always begin at the top left corner so that as the piece "grows" it will rest on the tabletop of the machine rather than pile up under the arm, in the way. (If you happen

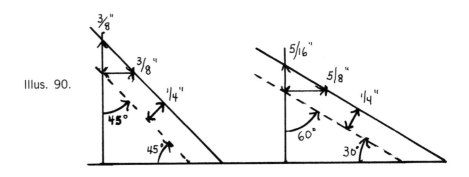

Illus. 90.

to be left-handed and prefer to sew with the seam allowance on the left side of the needle, however, then begin at the top right corner.)

Place the corner piece (which is the first piece in Row 1) right side up in front of the needle. Place the first piece for Row 2 right sides together on the other and sew the ¼" (.6cm) seam allowed. Use 12–14 stitches to the inch so that the stitches will hold during

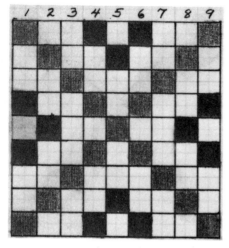

Illus. 91, Pattern 53. Diagram of chain-sewing.

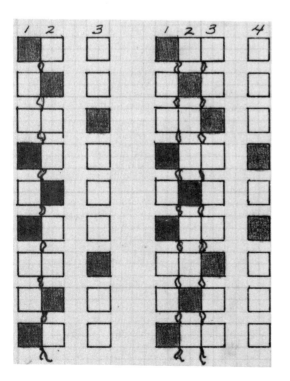

normal handling and no backstitches will be needed. At the end of this seam do not cut the thread, but pull out a short piece, perhaps ¼"–½" (.6cm–1.3cm), for spacing and get ready to sew the next two pairs.

Place the next piece down, in Row 1 right side up in front of the needle. Place the next piece down in Row 2, the right sides together on the other piece, and sew them. As before, leave a small space in the thread and continue to sew pairs of pieces as they are shown in the first two rows of the diagram. Sew all the pairs for the first two rows in this way. When opened they will then look like the drawing for Step 1—pieces stitched in pairs connected by the sewing threads. This is a chain of sewn pieces. The method used is called chain-sewing.

To these pairs add the pieces for Row 3, one at a time in the same way, beginning with the top piece in the row. These pieces are shown laid out beside the pieced pairs to which they will be stitched. When opened flat, the work will then look like the drawing for Step 2.

Beside that are the pieces for Row 4 which will be added next. Of course you will not need to lay out the pieces for each row in this way when you are sewing. Just keep the stacks of the various pieces at hand on a TV tray or something and select pieces as needed according to the diagram.

Continue to add pieces, row after row, following the diagram until all the rows have been added. Lay out the work and check the pieces to be sure that they are stitched in pattern according to the diagram.

Press the seam allowances by rows. Those in one row across will turn to the left. Those in the next row to the right.

Then fold the first row right sides together over the second and pin the seams exactly together. The seam allowances are already pressed in opposite directions. This also creates a little ridge on opposite sides of the seams. If you push these ridges one against the other and pin the seam allowance to be stitched first the seams will match exactly. You will develop a feel for this so that it will always happen.

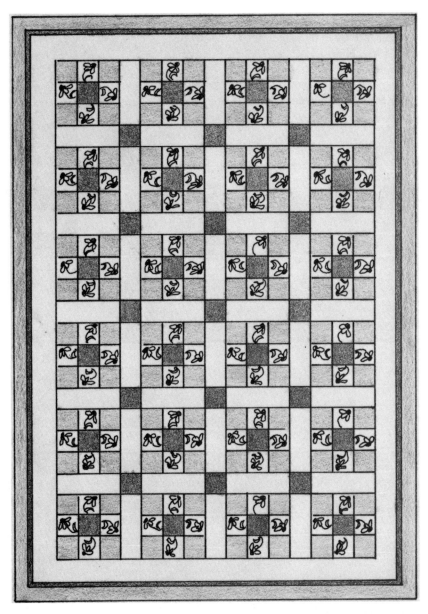

Illus. 92, Pattern 65. "Nine-patch."

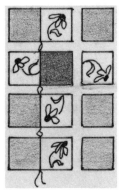

Do not, however, remove the pins as you stitch, for three reasons. The first is that if you remove the pin before you stitch over it the seams may slip and not match. So slow down as you approach a pin and "tiptoe" over it by turning the wheel by hand to make sure the needle does not hit the pin.

Secondly, having stitched over the pin, leave it in because it saves time not to stop to remove it.

The third reason is that as you pin the next edges for stitching each pin will be at hand as needed—no fishing for pins from a box or pincushion. Stitch all the cross-seams to complete the top. Press.

Chain-sewing not only saves time; it saves thread. It can be applied to the sewing of all types of pieces (even for garments!). The pieces of blocks can be chain-sewn. "Nine-patch" Illus. 92, Pattern 65, makes a good example for this. Begin with the first pieces at the top of the first two lengthwise rows of the block. Stitch them together as described before. Then chain-sew the next pair down, followed by the last pair for the block. This series of three pairs is enough of those pairs for one block, but do not cut the thread yet. Instead, continue to sew a series of these pairs for each block (in this case, 24) like the first one shown in Illus. 91.

When all are stitched start with the first series and add the pieces for the third lengthwise row to the pairs according to the diagram. Repeat this with each series of pairs until all the third row pieces have been chain-sewn.

As you press the seams, each row in the opposite direction, cut the long chains of pieces into block-sets to make them easier to handle when sewing the crossways seams for the blocks.

All square blocks made up of squares or other shapes can be sewn in this way. Blocks of strips such as for "Rail Fence" can also be chain-sewn.

Chain-sewing can apply to sewing numerous repeats of a single seam. Thus pieces of a block can be chain-sewn to form squares or strips or other portions of the block and then these can, in turn, be chain-sewn into blocks. As we go through the next few patterns I will indicate times when this can be done so that you will learn to look for them in all your other piecing as well.

Many of the blocks used in quilts are simply pieced squares, so they too can be chain-sewn whether they are set solid or with setting blocks. Just follow the diagram for the piecing order. See Illus. 93 for piecing nine-patch blocks.

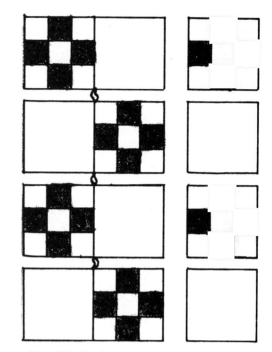

Illus. 93. Piecing diagram for chain-sewing nine-patch blocks with setting blocks.

If the blocks are to be set with short lattice strips and with squares at the corners, these too can be chain-sewn. See Illus. 94.

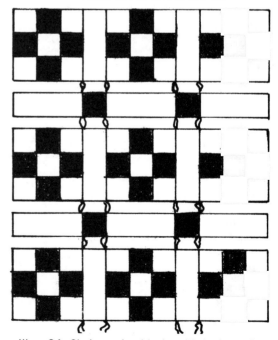

Illus. 94. Chain-sewing blocks with lattice strips and squares at corners.

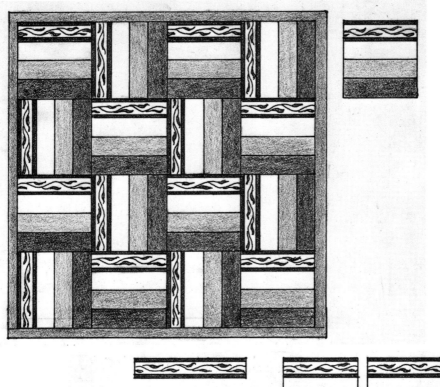

Some blocks must be correctly turned to form the desired allover pattern. Among these are Roman Stripe blocks. When turned one way they form "Rail Fence," Pattern 66 (Illus. 95); when arranged in a different order they make "Windmill," Pattern 67 (Illus. 96). The blocks for both patterns are the same, however. In piecing the blocks for both these patterns as shown, I first pieced a set of three strips, a print edged by two narrow solid colors, to create a stripe. Long segments of this set are chain-sewn with three other pieces to make the blocks. This touch of strip-piecing emphasizes the zigzag or windmill patterns in an interesting way.

Illus. 95, Pattern 66. "Rail Fence."

If the pattern is made on the scale usually used for quilting I stack three folded fabrics and cut six pieces (perhaps $2\frac{3}{4}'' \times 9\frac{1}{2}''$ or 7×24.2cm, including seam allowances) and then chain-sew them for the blocks. This way is faster and easier at this scale than the Seminole method of cutting segments of a set.

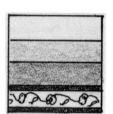

Illus. 96, Pattern 67. "Windmills."

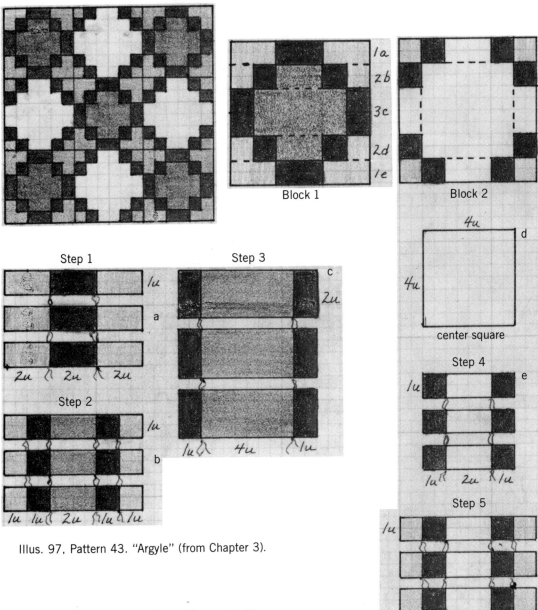

Illus. 97. Pattern 43. "Argyle" (from Chapter 3).

"Argyle" is Pattern 43 from Chapter 3. The allover design is created by piecing two different blocks which alternate in the rows of blocks across and down (Illus. 97). When pieced on a small scale, Seminole methods would be used, but for pieces of 1½" (3.8cm) or more I would cut stacks of pieces and chain-sew them.

For Block 1, I would chain-sew three different chains (a, b and c) as shown and then chain-sew the strips according to the diagram of the block.

For Block 2 I would chain-sew two chains (e and f) and then chain-sew two of the strips to opposite sides of Square d. Then I would chain-sew a group of Strip f and add these to the other opposite sides of Square d to complete the block.

Pattern 44, from Chapter 3, to which I have not yet given a name, presents a very involved piecing plan (Illus. 98). When it is done in sections, however, they are quite simple to do. If I were to piece this pattern on a small scale (1u = 1″ or 2.5cm) I might use the Seminole methods of sewing sets of strips and cutting segments.

For a 15″ (38.1cm) block (1u = 1½″ or 3.8cm) I would piece differently. As always, I would make a complete diagram of the quilt as a guide. Then the cutting of pieces could be done. I would fold and layer the three different fabrics needed for the small squares, marking and cutting stacks of six pieces (cut 2″ or 5.1cm size for this scale). Three different fabrics—white, light and medium on the diagram—are to be cut into rectangles of different sizes for each fabric. For each of these I would fold the fabric lengthwise and crossways to make four layers to be marked and cut into rectangles. I would fol-

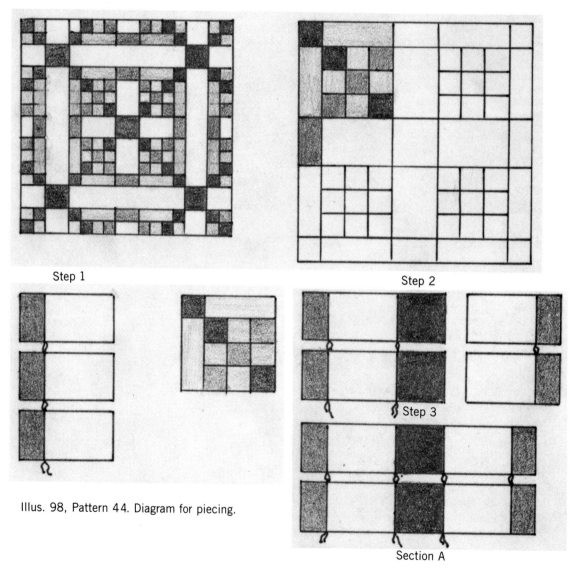

Step 1

Step 2

Step 3

Section A

Illus. 98, Pattern 44. Diagram for piecing.

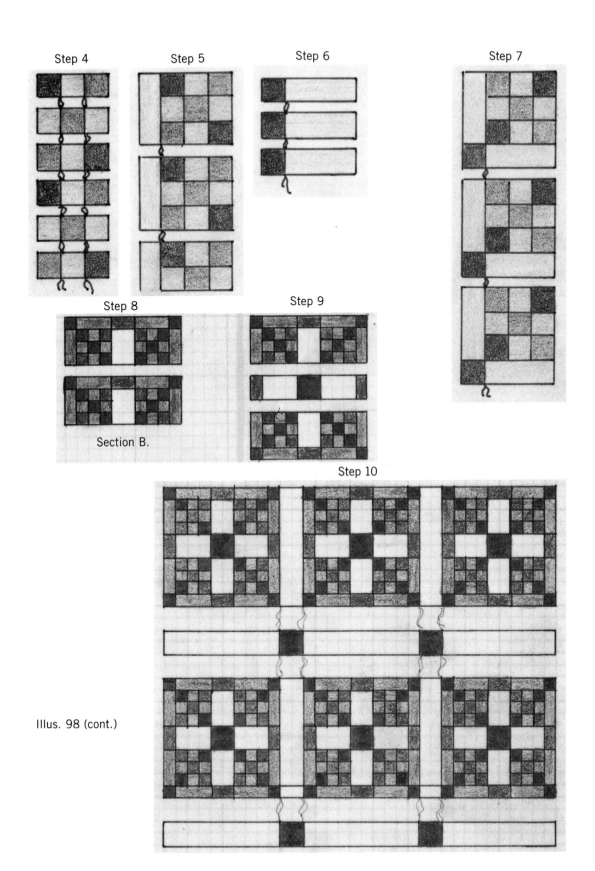

Step 4

Step 5

Step 6

Step 7

Step 8

Section B.

Step 9

Step 10

Illus. 98 (cont.)

low the same procedure with the fabric for the dark center square and the dark corner squares of the lattice. The white lattice rectangles can also be marked on four layers of fabric.

When all pieces were cut I would begin the piecing. Step 1 shows chain-sewing the two rectangles for the arms of the cross which dominates the block. Half of these "arms parts" are chain-sewn to opposite sides of the dark center square (Steps 2 & 3). This completes Section A.

The piecing of the corner part is begun by chain-sewing the small "Nine-patch" in Step 4. They are shown completed in Step 5, and light colored rectangles are chain-sewn to one side of them as shown. Make sure it is the side indicated in the diagram. The other light colored rectangles are chain-sewn to the rest of the small, dark squares in Step 6. These pairs of pieces are then chain-sewn to another side of the "Nine-patches" (Step 7). Again, make sure it is the side indicated in the diagram. This completes the corner parts.

Step 8 shows the sewing of corner parts to opposite sides of the remaining arm parts to complete the piecing of the B sections.

In Step 9, B sections are chain-sewn on each side of an A section to finish the blocks. That done, there only remains the chain-sewing of the blocks with the lattice parts as seen in the diagram.

Pattern 68, Illus. 99, is an old design named "Clay's Choice." It is included to show a piecing situation different from any we have yet considered. Pieces of various shapes are stitched together as a unit and four of these units are turned, each in a different position, to form the block. This piecing method can be employed for innumerable patterns so it is well to form the habit of learning to see these parts of the block as it is studied for piecing.

The usual appearance of "Clay's Choice," is shown at the upper left corner of the Illustration. On the right is my variation. I have cut segments of a pieced strip to use as the diamond-shaped pieces in the pattern.

This pieced strip is 3u wide (not including

the seam allowances). A template 2u wide plus seam allowances is made and laid on the strip at a 45° angle to the edge. The template should be made long enough for both sides to reach across the strip. It should be laid on the right side of the strips at the angle shown; otherwise the stripes will run in the other direction across the diamond.

The squares in the pattern also measure 2u (remember that this type of measure does not include seam allowances. They must be added.) The squares will be marked on a single layer of fabric and sewn in pairs to the fabric laid right sides together under the marked fabric by the method described earlier in this chapter. Chain-sew four pair for each block to be made. See Step 1.

Make a paper pattern of this same size square, 2u (do not include seam allowances) and use it in the method described for marking half-square triangles on the fabric. This time the triangles are cut out first and then chain-sewn to opposite sides of the pieced diamonds as shown in Step 2 to form a rectangle the same size as that made by the two pieced squares. The two rectangles are chain-sewn to form the units which are chain-sewn to make the blocks.

The next pattern, #69 (Illus. 100), is called "Whirlwind." It is included to show the marking of pieces on the fabric with the aid of a template used in a slightly different way than I have seen before.

With this pattern also, I have enhanced the dominant piece with strip piecing. I have included three ways of doing this for one pattern to stimulate your thinking along these lines, for it can be applied effectively to many simple patterns. By this I do not imply that simple patterns are not attractive—far from it. This is just one way of creating variations—a practice dear to the hearts of quiltmakers!

The method for drafting this pattern by folding paper is shown with Variation 1 of "Whirlwind" in Step 1. Cut a square of the size desired for the block. Fold it from edge to edge of the paper in all the directions shown by the dashed lines, creasing the folds well to define them. On this same sketch,

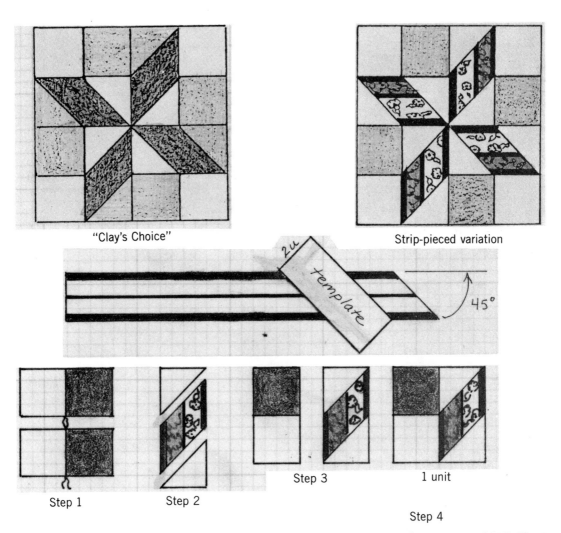

"Clay's Choice"

Strip-pieced variation

Step 1

Step 2

Step 3

1 unit

Step 4

Illus. 99, Pattern 68. "Clay's Choice."

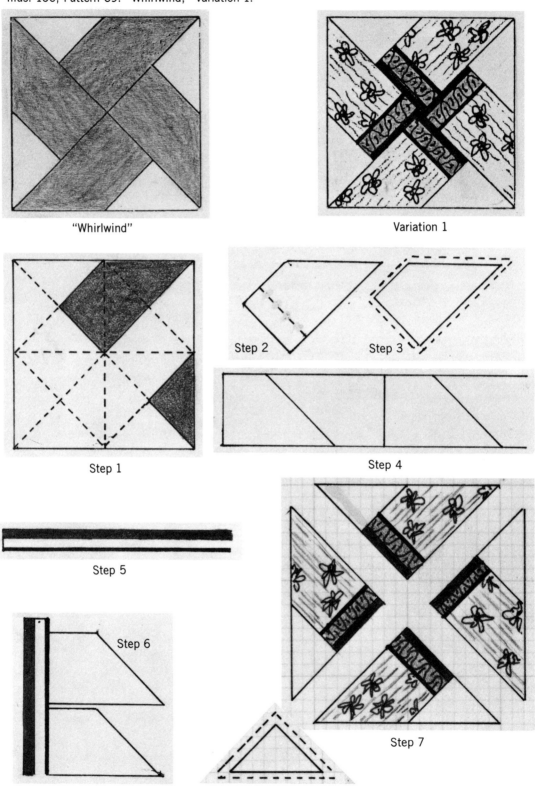

Illus. 100, Pattern 69. "Whirlwind," Variation 1.

"Whirlwind"

Variation 1

Step 1

Step 2

Step 3

Step 4

Step 5

Step 6

Step 7

94

two areas are shaded in. They indicate the two pieces used for the block. Carefully cut out one piece of each shape and use it to draw a pattern on paper. Use a ruler to make the lines straight. Lay the triangular piece aside for use later. Mark off a part near the square end of the other piece (which is a trapezoid) as wide as you would like the pieced strip to be (Step 2) and cut it off.

The pieced strip I have used is made of a wide print strip bordered by narrow ones. Any number (even one!) and width of strips that please you can be used—try your own ideas! Add seam allowances to the width of the piece to be strip pieced.

Add ¼″ (.6cm) seam allowances all around the trapezoid pattern after the piece is cut off (Step 3). Then measure across the end of the piece. Use that measurement to mark strips across your fabric. The fabric must not be folded for cutting because this would reverse the pieces cut off the second layer. Several layers can be cut, however, by cutting the fabric into shorter lengths (½ or ¼, etc.) and stacking all the layers right-side-up.

Make a template of the pattern and use it to mark the fabric. To do this lay the template between the lines of the marked strips and mark the ends of the pieces as shown in Step 4. This is faster and more accurate than marking all around the template for each piece.

The sketch shows the template as it should be positioned if it is laid on the *right* side of the fabric. If you prefer to mark the wrong side, turn the template over as well as the fabric, otherwise the pinwheel shape will spin in the opposite direction from that shown. I see no reason why this situation would be less desirable than the other, but you should be aware of what would happen. Pin the marked pieces, if they are layered, and cut them out.

Piece your set of strips as planned (Step 5) and then strip-stitch the pieces to the pieced set (Step 6). Before pressing this seam hold the piece firmly in place, or pin it as you prefer, and cut the strip to fit. Then press.

Draw a paper pattern of the triangular piece cut, adding seam allowances all around (Step 7). Follow the instructions earlier in

this chapter for working with half-square triangles. Using the measurement of this triangle as indicated in those instructions, mark and cut the fabric for triangles (it may be folded one or more times with no problem).

Chain-sew the triangles to the top of the pieces (trapezoids) just finished to form a triangular unit. Then chain-sew these triangles to make the block (Step 8). All sides of the block will be bias.

In my second variation of "Whirlwind" (Illus. 101) I have made a wide set of strips from which the entire trapezoid is cut. Make your patterns in the same way as for the first variation and cut out the shaded triangular pieces. A quarter-square triangle will be needed so follow the instructions for making them.

Make a template of the other piece without cutting any away, but do include the seam allowances (Step 1). Measure across the template at the place indicated by the arrows on the drawing and use this measurement for the width of the set of pieced strips.

Lay the template on the right side of the set as shown in the drawing and mark the pieces (Step 2). When they are cut the triangles can be added and the blocks completed as for Variation 1. For this variation the block edge will be with the grain, but all seams within it will be bias.

You will not want to waste the triangular pieces of the set which were left from cutting the pieces for the block. I found a use for mine by strip-stitching the triangles to a strip of dark fabric by the usual method (not shown here) so that when I sewed my triangles to make squares the little blocks would have a dark frame. These small squares can be stitched with or without lattice and used for any small quilting piece, such as a pillow. One square, if it were lined, would make a pretty pocket for an apron or a child's dress.

Variation 3 (Illus. 102) is the pattern for the red and navy quilt on the cover of the book. I have not seen this setting for the pattern before. I began by making a diagram of the quilt to be sure that the blocks would work together as I imagined, and to use as a guide in the usual ways.

Illus. 101, Pattern 69. "Whirlwind," Variation 2.

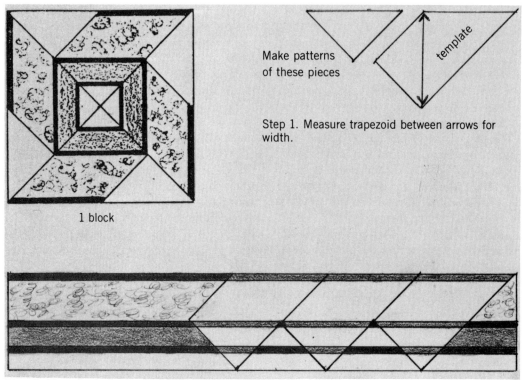

Make patterns
of these pieces

template

Step 1. Measure trapezoid between arrows for width.

1 block

Step 2. Pieced set of strips marked with template.

I drafted my patterns on graph paper and made my template in the way described for Variation 2. To find the width for the set of strips for this version I measured across the square end of the template.

I cut crossways strips of fabric and stitched them into sets. Then I pressed the seam allowances of half the sets in one direction and those of the other half in the other direction. This pressing should be gently done to keep from distorting the strips.

The template was used to mark the shapes

Illus. 102. Use triangles saved from cutting pieces in Step 2 to piece squares for some other quilting project, such as a pillow.

Illus. 103, Pattern 69. "Whirlwind," Variation 3 ("Whirlwind Point").

Block 1

Block 2

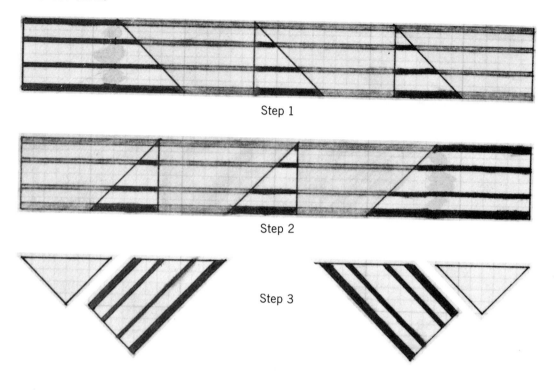

Step 1

Step 2

Step 3

on the set. Half of the pieces, all with seam allowances pressed in the same direction, are marked with the template in the position for Block 1 (Step 1). Before marking the other half I turned the template over to the position for Part 2 (Step 2). In this case I marked and cut each piece singly. (The small triangles left from this cutting can be pieced into squares which are miniature versions of "Whirlwind.")

Unbleached muslin was chosen for the triangles to be added to the pieces just cut. They were marked and cut by the method for half-squares, and stitched to the trapezoid pieces just as in the other variations of this pattern. The units formed were then chain-sewn into blocks. The way that the set of strips was marked and cut, using the template in two positions, reversed half the pieces, thus insuring that I would have two different blocks, one the reverse of the other, when finished.

The sides of these blocks are bias, which

presents a challenge when they are sewn together. The pressing of the pieced strips was done in such a way as to make the seam allowances lie in opposite directions when these seams are sewn. This helps in matching the seams of the strips so that the points formed by them are accurate. This takes care of one piecing challenge.

The challenge of the bias seams may present a problem to some. If so, mark the block measurement (in my quilt 10½" or 26.7cm, including seam allowances) on paper or tear-away Pellon® and pin the edges of two matched blocks between the marks, gently patting and smoothing away any stretching. Sew the blocks and tear off the paper or Pellon®.

Following the diagram, Blocks 1 and 2 were sewn alternately both across and down the quilt forming the interesting allover patterns of chevrons as designed.

The border was simple to add. I consulted my diagram for the measurement of the

width to cut and for the number of blocks across and down. For the side borders I figured the length of the border strip by multiplying the number of blocks in the length by the block measurement (10″ or 25.4cm). Then I added twice the width of the border plus 2″ (5.1cm) because I like a little extra length for handling. I followed the same procedure for the end borders and then marked and cut both, two at a time, on fabric folded once lengthwise and twice crossways (8 layers).

On each border piece I began at the middle and placed pins all along the border strip to mark the measurement of the block. Then I pinned the blocks to the border, matching the block seams to the pins. Between them I smoothed the bias edges of the block to fit the correct measurement and pinned as needed. I marked, with a pin, a point at each corner of the pieced top which was exactly ¼″ (.6cm) from both edges. I stuck the pin through the border at this point and set my machine needle there to begin my sewing. I stitched (¼″ or .6cm seam) with the border on top to cover the bias edge of the pieced top. When I got to the other end of my seam, I stopped at the pin, turned the wheel to raise the thread uptake bar just past the highest point (to prevent puckering) and then backstitched a few stitches. I tied the threads at the other end. I repeated this process for

each border piece and pressed the seam allowances towards the borders.

I took the quilt to the cutting board and laid out one corner area smoothly with edges along lines of the board. I extended the end of one border out straight and pinned it to the board. Then I turned under the end of the adjoining piece at a diagonal and laid it so that the edges of both ends lay exactly together (Illus. 104), and I pinned them in place. Then I brought my hot iron to the cutting board and carefully pressed a crease where the top border end was folded under. I lifted the quilt on that border side and pinned the crease.

I repeated this process with the other three corners before I took the quilt back to the machine and stitched along the creases, backstitching or tying the threads at the ends of the stitching. The crease began at the end of the border seam, so the two border seams and the crease seam came together at the same point. After I had checked this, I trimmed the mitre seams to ¼″ (.6cm) and the top was finished.

The last pattern in this chapter is "Nelson's Victory" (Illus. 105, Pattern 70). I have varied this pattern also with strip piecing. It is included to demonstrate setting in squares.

The pattern is drafted by folding a paper square as indicated by the dashed lines in the

Illus. 105, Pattern 70. "Nelson's Victory."

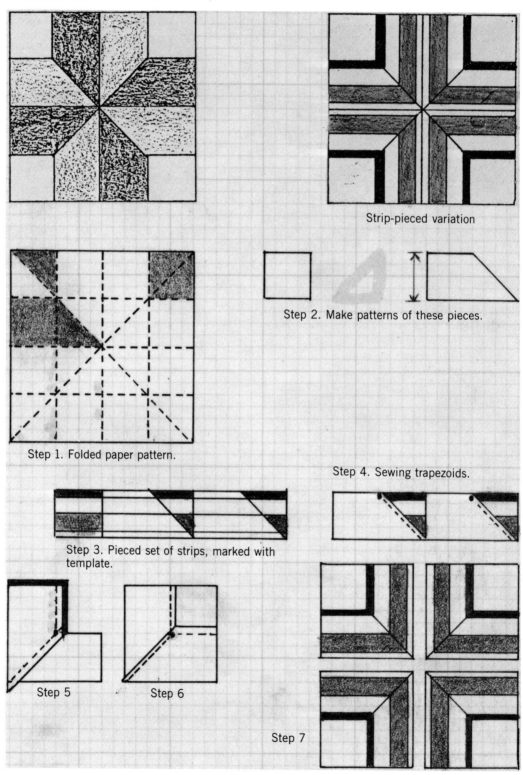

Strip-pieced variation

Step 2. Make patterns of these pieces.

Step 1. Folded paper pattern.

Step 4. Sewing trapezoids.

Step 3. Pieced set of strips, marked with template.

Step 5   Step 6

Step 7

diagram (Step 1). The shaded areas in the drawing show the various shapes for the pattern (Step 2).

Only the square and the trapezoid are needed. The triangle is shown for those who do not want to set in squares. If that is the case, cut half-square triangles, sew them to the trapezoid, and finish piecing the block in the obvious way, chain-sewing, of course.

The measurement for the set of pieced strips for this pattern is found by measuring the end of the template you should make of the trapezoid as described in Variation 2 for Pattern 69. Piece the set (Step 3) and press the seam allowances as for Variation 3 of that pattern. Reverse pieces will be needed of the trapezoid but this time we will try a different method of producing them.

With the template, mark the pieces as shown, *but* mark the wrong side of half the sets of strips only. Pin the other half of the sets right sides together to the first group. The seam allowances are already lying in opposite directions to help in matching the strip seams. Pin each place where the seams must match along the diagonal line drawn for that end of the piece. Sew ¼" (.6cm) from the diagonal line but stop ¼" (.6cm) from the edge as indicated in the drawing by the dot at the end of the stitching line (Step 4). Backstitch as was done previously.

Cut the stitched pieces apart and save the leftover triangles for piecing small squares for another project. Press the diagonal seam allowance in either direction but take care not to stretch it.

Cut the squares by methods described previously in this chapter. Match one square to the edge of one of the sewn pair of pieces just cut, as is shown in Step 5. Sew a ¼" (.6cm) seam as shown stopping at the end of

the diagonal seam as indicated by the dot. Backstitch. The diagonal seam was stopped at this point to allow for matching the adjoining side of the square to the edge of the other trapezoid joined by the diagonal seam. Pin and stitch this seam, again stopping at the dot as indicated. Press these last two seams towards the square. This completes one of four units needed for the block. These can be chain-sewn.

In this chapter I have described the basic methods which I use in making quilt tops of different types of patterns. The use of the diagram as a guide for all phases of the piecing project from the planning through the final stitching of the border has been strongly emphasized. This aid is helpful to the experienced piecer as well as to the beginner.

After explaining some of the more basic methods, I began to apply them to the piecing of patterns as an example of how I use them. I started with a method for piecing a pattern of simple squares by following a diagram. Then I demonstrated that this is a basic method to piecing tops, by showing that in many cases pieced blocks are simply pieced squares. Thus they can be pieced into tops following the diagram. It was seen further that even lattices, which are not squares, can be handled by this same method in piecing the top.

A number of different patterns were used to demonstrate methods for handling various situations which arise in the piecing of patterns. An easy way to piece a mitred border accurately was included.

The methods explained in this chapter will be referred to in those which follow. As other patterns are presented, some other methods will be included with them from time to time.

5

Adapting Seminole Piecing

The idea of using Seminole patterns to make quilts is not new. The few examples I have seen have all been made with a variety of pieced bands of the types seen in Chapter 2. In the quilts I saw, these bands were much enlarged in scale, of course, and were separated by unpieced bands of varying widths. Only solid colors were used throughout the quilts. This is a direct translation from the Seminole use of pattern. The quilts were very attractive, but the effect, to me, was the same as when I saw an example of a delicate petit point design worked also on rug canvas. The pattern was the same, but the change in scale had somewhat changed the spirit of the piece so that it was now a bold statement where it had been a sensitive interpretation.

These quilts in Seminole patterns reminded me of "stripey" quilts, which are also made by alternating plain and pieced bands. In the stripey quilts, however, the patterns are patchwork, of course, and the fabrics are often prints or prints mixed with solid colors.

Making quilts in this manner with enlarged bands of Seminole patterns is a legitimate adaptation, to be sure, and an obvious one as well. It is not my intent to discourage the practice. Those who have been involved with it have, so far as I know, also done the piecing by the same methods developed for the small-scale patterns; and it is this that I question.

Happily the stripey quilt, attractive as it is,

is not the only alternative for the use of Seminole design in making quilts; and that is what this chapter is all about.

Most of the patterns found in Chapter 2, as well as from numerous other sources, are well suited for use as border patterns. Borders have a strong appeal for today's quilters. The growing popularity of medallion quilts encourages this interest because that type of top presents opportunities for using a number of borders. When some of these borders are pieced of small patterns, they make a pleasing contrast to those of larger scale or to those of plain strips of fabric.

It is my feeling that one should no more hesitate to mix Seminole patterns with those of traditional patchwork than one would question the appropriateness of mixing different periods and styles of home furnishings and other art forms used in decorating. Good design of any period or culture, when combined with sensitivity, can be intermixed to achieve pleasing effects. One notable example of this which I have recently seen was a gleaming coffee service on an antique dresser placed against a rough log cabin wall. The rich blending of textures and styles stimulated such an awareness of the differing historic settings which had produced each one that they produced a very poignant atmosphere.

In selecting Seminole patterns for a border, the same challenges are presented as when other types of patterns are used. Attention must be given to the scale of any pattern and the colors to be used for it and indeed to the type of pattern—whether it is to be simple or elaborate. These characteristics must be considered in relationship to the same qualities of other patterns, borders or parts of any type which are planned for the quilt top. Each element, though separate, must be considered as an individual unit and as a portion of the complete quilt top, for the smallest change in one part will affect every other part of the top as well as the finished appearance.

There are some lovely quilts, it is true, which have "just grown" from stage to stage. That happy conclusion is not always the case, however. Generally speaking, it is more practical and reassuring to plan carefully on paper before beginning to cut fabric, especially if the quilt is to be of an elaborate design. Even then it is impossible to judge every time exactly how a certain color or print or scale will

work together with others because it is not possible to produce exact colors, prints and scales on paper. It is only possible to get a general idea of the potential effect. One must be prepared to take out any part that does not work well even though it is already sewn in. The fabric or patchwork removed can likely be salvaged for another project.

Some designers try to keep this necessity to a minimum by pinning samples of fabrics of the planned size to a large bulletin board on the wall so that they can stand back and evaluate the effect of all parts together. You may want to try something of this sort if you are, or become, sufficiently involved in this type of quilting.

Plain borders can easily be measured and cut to fit any length and width desired. A patterned one is another matter. Some patterns lend themselves easily to the length and width of the area allotted to them, while others do not. A repeated pattern, whether printed or pieced, must fit exactly into the

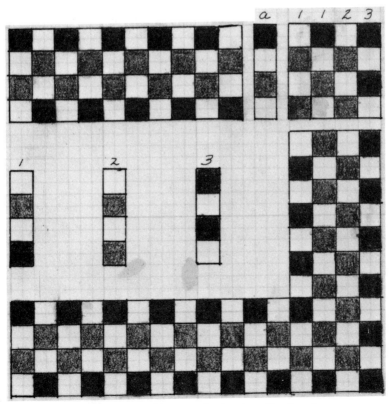

Illus. 106, Pattern 71. Diagram of a border with pieced corner.

length allowed with no fractions of a repeat left over. This is one of the places where the unit measurements used in this book will help you to scale up or down to fit a space. In fitting in a repeat of a pattern do not forget that in some instances a portion of a repeat is needed at the end of the length for balance.

Illus. 106 shows an equal repeat of the pattern of segments. To achieve a balance in the pattern, however, a Segment a must be added. This is also required for all the corners to be the same. Corners are sometimes included in the figuring of repeats and at other times are not, depending upon the pattern and how it is to be handled at the corner.

The way a border will turn a corner is always of importance. Probably the easiest patterns to handle are those of segments which were cut straight across the set and then stitched in, alternately reversing positions to form the band. These can simply be mitred at the corners. The way the pieces come together in the process often creates interesting patterns. Three examples of this are shown in Illus. 107.

If sets are pieced of strips which are all the same width, and if the segments are cut that width also, the pattern of the band has a checkered appearance. These bands can also be mitred, but there is another way to handle

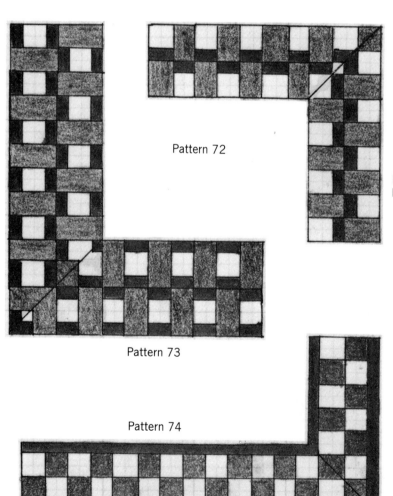

Pattern 72

Illus. 107, Patterns 72–74.
Borders with mitred corners.

Pattern 73

Pattern 74

104

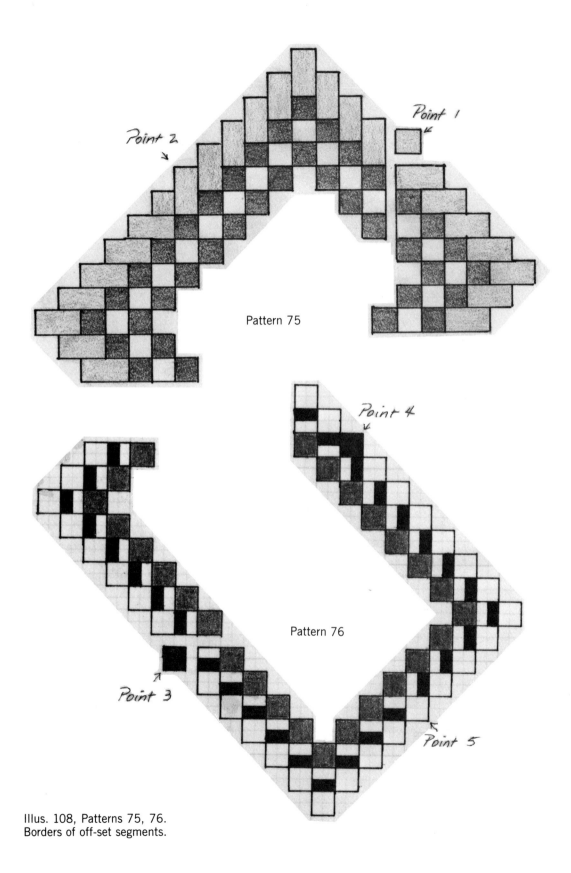

Point 1

Point 2

Pattern 75

Point 4

Point 3

Pattern 76

Point 5

Illus. 108, Patterns 75, 76.
Borders of off-set segments.

105

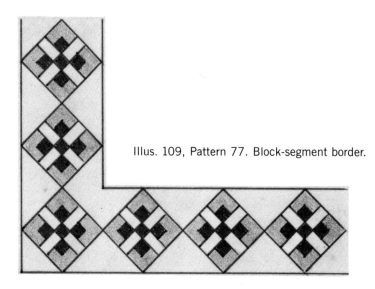

Illus. 109, Pattern 77. Block-segment border.

them at the corners which appears to be more natural. A few sets may be pieced especially to suit the needs of the design as it goes around the corner. One or more segments of each set are pieced into a square which forms the corner and fits into the pattern of the borders smoothly. Illus. 108 shows how this is done.

Those bands which are pieced of segments cut straight across the set of strips (of any width) and are sewn together in an off-set position make very attractive borders. The width of the segments must be the same as the step up or down from one segment to the next in the band. The corners for this type of band or border are easily handled. They will simply continue at the same angle at the corner but the step up becomes a step down. To keep the corners all alike, however, a reverse of the direction of the slant of the segments must occur at the middle of the border as shown in Illus. 108. A little adjustment in the piecing is required to make a smooth transition.

In Pattern 75, the design flows smoothly all around even though the segments change their slant at the middle of the border. To achieve this appearance, a few squares are removed from some segments at Point 1 and one square is added to fill in the pattern at the outside edge.

The transition in Pattern 76 can be handled in one of two ways according to preference. The dark squares added at Points 3 and 4 emphasize the change. At Point 5 the white square added is not noticeable so the change is only indicated by the slant of the small rectangles where the reverse occurs.

Bands made of block-segments (Illus. 109) can be handled in very much the same way as the type just considered. These segments also progress with a step up or down which is the same measurement as the width of the segment. The step up to the corner becomes a step down afterwards. No reversal of the slant of the segments is required along the border, however. Instead, a square of the same fabric used to set the blocks is added at two opposite corners to fill in the point. The row of little squares set on the diagonal makes a particularly attractive border. Choose the symmetrical blocks for borders. The diagonal ones do not turn the corner well.

A border of chevron bands is especially effective and the way it turns the corner enhances the design (Illus. 110). A little planning is required to achieve this. First, the two segments which are mitred at the corner must be cut twice as wide as usual to allow enough width for the mitre. I find that I usually do not need quite this much width for

Illus. 110, Pattern 78. Chevron band border.

the mitre to be stitched as shown, but any extra is easily trimmed off. Second, a half-square triangle is needed to fill in the point of the corner. This could be cut of the same fabric as used for the segments at the outside of the border. An interesting alternative might be to cut this triangle of the fabric which will be stitched along the outside of the border. This choice would emphasize the corner turning of the chevron design.

Unfortunately certain types of patterns do not lend themselves to turning corners. Among these are bands in which the slant of the segments in relation to the edge of the band is at any angle other than 45°. These

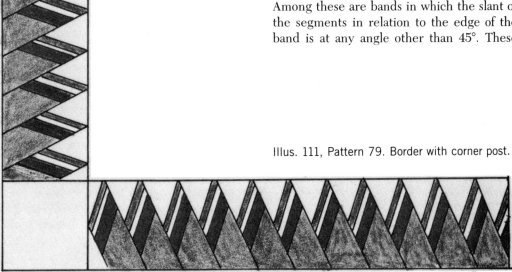

Illus. 111, Pattern 79. Border with corner post.

Illus. 112, Pattern 80. Seminole center.

Illus. 114, Pattern 82. "Seminole Star II."

Illus. 113, Pattern 81. "Seminole Star I."

applied this to the making of borders but we are not through with them yet. These blocks can be used in the small scale in which they are traditionally made by simply substituting one or more of them for patches in a patchwork block. The center square of a "Nine-patch" might be one of these pieced Seminole blocks. In Illus. 112–114, three block choices are suggested. If one is feeling more ambitious, the four corner squares might be replaced by the little blocks instead of, or in addition to, the center one.

If you are thinking that this is a lot of work, remember that "Double Nine-patch" has five pieced squares. Also remember that the Seminole methods of piecing make the work faster and easier. This suggestion for using little Seminole squares would consume no more time and energy than the traditional piecing of "Double Nine-patch"—possibly not as much.

The same idea can be applied to numerous other patterns as effectively as to "Nine-patch." I have used Seminole Pattern 18 (Illus. 28, Chapter 2) in the center of an "Ohio Star" block to make a variation I call "Seminole Star I." (Pattern 81, Illus. 173) Pattern 16 (Illus. 76, Chapter 2) is used as the center of "Variable Star" for a variation I have named "Seminole Star II" (Pattern 8, Illus.

patterns are very appealing, however, in spite of this difficulty. A possible solution to this problem is to use a square as a corner piece, like a fence post. (Illus. 111) The pattern then runs from post to post. Other "posts" might be spaced along the border as part of the design if desired.

In adapting Seminole patterns for use in quilting, stripey quilts and borders are only a beginning. The small-block patterns, which are sewn into block segments, are the next most logical area to explore. We have already

Illus. 115. Three settings of Pattern 16 from Chapter 2.

14). Any pattern of squares which is fairly simple, so that the little Seminole squares will show off to advantage, might be considered for this treatment.

In Chapter 2, attention was called to the fact that Seminole squares or blocks are very similar to quilt blocks and in a few cases are exactly the same. They can, therefore, be enlarged to quilt block size and used in the same ways as the usual quilt blocks are used.

Illus. 116. Three settings of Pattern 17 from Chapter 2.

Illus. 117. Four settings of Pattern 18 from Chapter 2.

Illus. 118. Two variations of
Pattern 20 from Chapter 2.
One is with lattice, and one is
with setting blocks.

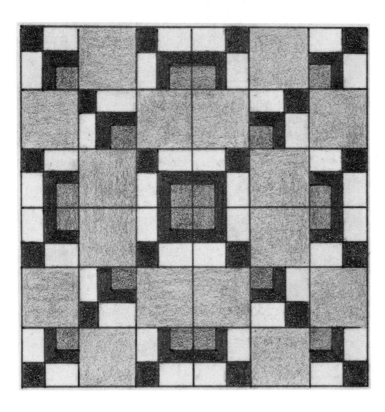

Illus. 119, Pattern 21, shown with lattice only.

The patterns which are symmetrical are more like those we are used to piecing for our quilts. I have chosen three of these and drawn diagrams of them set solid as well as with lattice and with setting blocks to show how they would look made that way into quilts. All are from Chapter 2. Illus. 115 is Pattern 16 (from Illus. 26). Illus. 116 is Pattern 17 (from Illus. 27) and Illus. 117 is Pattern 18 (from Illus. 28).

Though quilters are not accustomed to working with block designs with a diagonal emphasis, these patterns too are quite applicable to quilting and create interesting all-over patterns whether they are set solid or are pieced with lattice or setting blocks. A number of these types of patterns also have been selected for diagramming to show the effects, which can be created with asymmetrical blocks.

Pattern 20 (Illus. 118) is shown set with lattice and with setting blocks.

Pattern 21 (Illus. 119) is shown with lattice only.

Pattern 22 (Illus. 120 and 121) is shown set solid and with lattice.

Pattern 23 (Illus. 122–124) is shown in two different color-shading combinations, each to show the difference this can make.

Pattern 24 (Illus. 125) is drawn with lattice.

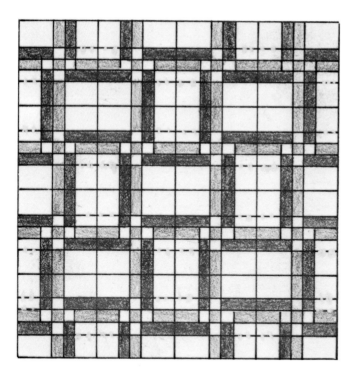

Illus. 120, Pattern 22, Variation 1.

Illus. 121, Pattern 22, Variation 2.

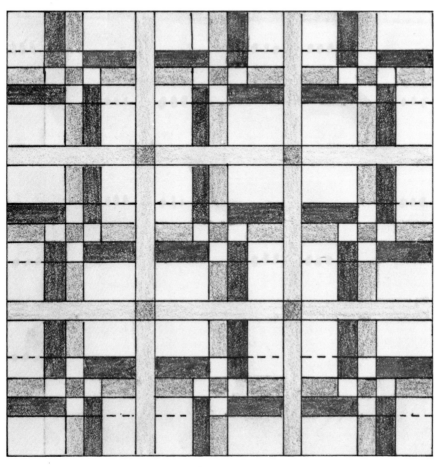

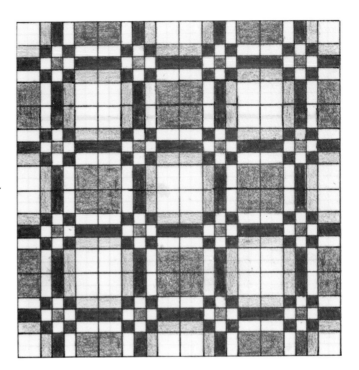

Illus. 122, Pattern 23, Variation 1.

Illus. 123, Pattern 23, Variation 2.

Illus. 124A, Pattern 23, Variation 3, set solid.

Obviously these patterns are readily adaptable for piecing quilts. With a little study of the blocks and the color-shading variations which are presented with them in Chapter 2, you see that I have shown only a few of the possibilities for using these patterns in this way. If you try to work with them, soon you'll be discovering designs of your own.

In addition to these ways of setting quilt blocks, quilters also enjoy finding two different patterns which work well together in a quilt. Pattern 82, Illus. 126, which I call Seminole Blossom uses two Seminole blocks with setting block to make up the design. This idea can be used for many other combinations as well.

Shown next in Illus. 127 is an arrangement of four blocks of Pattern 25, from Chap. 2, set together to form the design. If the pattern is pieced on the scale of ½u = 1″ or 2.5cm, the four blocks would measure 13″ (33.0cm), a good size for a pillow. If the scale is 1u = 1″ (2.5cm), the piece would measure 26″ (66.0cm) without border. This would be a good size for a small wall hanging. That same scale is appropriate for a quilt-size piece. It would be very effective made up in that size.

When Seminole patterns are enlarged for

Illus. 124B, Pattern 23, Variation 4, set with lattice.

Illus. 125, Pattern 24, with lattice.

Illus. 126, Pattern 82. "Seminole Blossom."

piecing as quilt blocks, as we have done in this chapter, the same piecing methods which were developed especially for piecing them on a small scale can still be used.

It has been my experience, however, that the cutting and piecing methods I described in Chapter 4 are more time-saving when large pieces are involved. Some of the methods I use are my own adaptations of Seminole methods. I do sew long strips together and later cut them up into segments. (I do this for example when I am working with only two fabrics which are to be of pieces stitched in pairs.) But when I do this, I always mark the length of the pieces to be cut at the time that I mark the strips because it saves time to do this at that time with a yardstick rather than to do it later with a template. It is also more accurate. In addition, I sew those strips before I cut them, which is another of my time-saving variations.

The Seminole method which I call strip-stitching and which was diagrammed for Pattern 12 is another one that I like to use with larger patterns.

If you have studied what I have written

Illus. 127, Pattern 25.

about my approach to piecing together with the illustrations and diagrams used in the previous chapters as well as this one you should have no trouble piecing all these designs without detailed instructions. It is a lot to learn if you are a beginner. Some practice with the various methods, as you work on one piecing project after another, will soon make them your own. When this happens it will give you a freedom of selection in your piecing and improved finished pieces as a reward for your efforts. When this is the case, then one purpose of this book as it relates to you shall have been achieved.

6
Expanding Strip-Piecing

This chapter is, in a sense, an extension of Chapters 2 and 3 because the designs presented here grew out of an interest in strip-piecing methods and an exploration of their application. It was felt, however, that the information in Chapters 4 and 5 should be introduced between those chapters and this one because it would prepare the reader to use the patterns in Chapter 6 with greater understanding and ease.

The actual dividing of the patterns into the various chapters has, in many cases, been a difficult decision, for numerous ones were appropriate in more than one chapter. So it happens that some of the patterns which were planned for this chapter were borrowed to be used as examples in Chapter 3 to illustrate a line of developing ideas. In Chapter 4, my strip-pieced variations of several patterns, which would have been in this chapter, are used in diagramming piecing methods rather than using the conventional examples of "Rail Fence," "Clay's Choice" or "Whirlwind" to name a few.

In Chapter 6, I have diagrammed a number of patterns for your piecing pleasure. Several are designs shown in Chapter 3 which developed as a result of my interest in strip-piecing. There are a number of patterns which have been enhanced by sets of pieced strips in one way or another. There are also designs which developed from Seminole patterns and have been expanded for use in quilting.

Illus. 128 shows Pattern 29 from Chapter 3 as a small quilt. It is one of the earliest patterns in which I used that persistent little three-piece strip with which I was involved for so long a time. At first it was named simply "Stepping Stones," until I saw another quite different pattern with that name. I then called it "Stepping Stones Around the World," partly to distinguish it from that other pattern but also because of the arrangement of the blocks. The fact that I was piecing a small "Trip Around the World" quilt had an influence, too, perhaps.

A study of the blocks for the design shows it to be a Roman Stripe variation since that was the pattern which inspired my three-piece set.

Five different square blocks are required to piece the pattern. The different color combinations and the way the blocks are turned create the rectangular shapes in the design. In my design, Block 1 is a strip of unbleached muslin bordered by dark brown. It appears horizontally and only across the middle of the quilt as the center block and every other horizontal block on each side of it.

Block 2 has dark brown borders on a tiny print of brown, rust, yellow and white.

Block 3 has muslin between a dark brown strip and a pumpkin (orange-rust) strip. These also are used only horizontally.

Block 4 used the pumpkin strips to border the same tiny print used in Block 2.

Block 5 alternates horizontally with Block 1

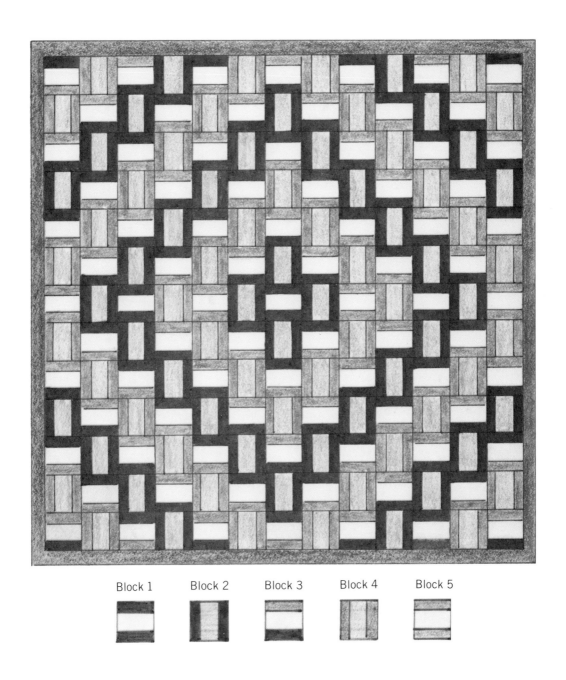

Block 1   Block 2   Block 3   Block 4   Block 5

Illus. 128, Pattern 29. "Stepping Stones Around the World."

across the middle row of blocks. Muslin is bordered by the pumpkin borders for this block.

The rectangular stepping stones are of two color combinations. The dark ones are formed because the dark brown strip of a Block 3 is stitched at each end of Block 2 which has two dark brown borders. The pumpkin strip is stitched to each end of Block 4 to make the other stepping stones.

Illus. 129, Pattern 33. "Nine-patch Plus."

"Nine-patch Plus" (Illus. 129, Pattern 33 from Chapter 3) uses the three-strip segments as "Nine-patch" patches. For this quilt block 1u = 1″ or 2.5cm, so the middle strip is 2″ or 5.1cm (+ seam allowances = 2½″) and the side strips are 1″ or 2.5cm (cut 1½″ or 3.8cm wide). The length of the segment is cut 4½″ (11.4cm) long. This measurement was marked on all the middle strips when the strip lines were marked. The strips were then stitched and the previously marked segment lengths were used to cut all three pieces.

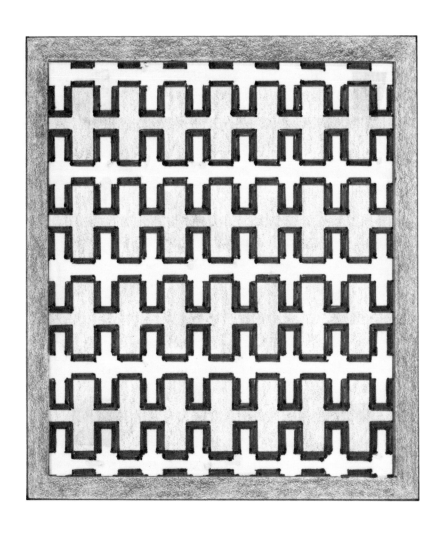

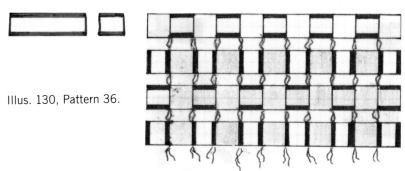

Illus. 130, Pattern 36.

The 4½″ (11.4cm) patches formed in this way were chain-sewn with plain patches to piece the two different blocks shown in the diagram. The blocks were then chain-sewn alternately to complete the top.

Pattern 36 from Chapter 3 is shown in Illus. 130 as it would appear if pieced for a quilt. This time the three-strip segments are arranged in a stripe pattern. Piece the set and cut segments as usual then chain-sew pieced

Illus. 131, Pattern 83. "Clockworks."

and unpieced patches alternately, following your diagram to make sure the pieced patches are turned in the correct position. The stripe can be used horizontally or vertically.

Illus. 131, Pattern 83, "Clockworks" looks like a very complicated design but is actually quite simple to piece. It developed from "Windmill," seen in Chapter 4, Illus. 96 Pattern 67. In this design there are only three

strips to the two different blocks. Both have an unpieced middle strip. One of the side strips has a triangle pieced at one end. The other has triangles at both ends.

Make a pattern of the half-square triangle by the methods in Chapter 4. Mark and cut layers of fabric triangles.

Make templates of the other piece in each side strip. These are both trapezoids since they are four-sided figures with two parallel

Illus. 132, Pattern 84. "Lanterns in the Night." Piecing diagram is on the following page.

sides. The shapes are not the same as those you have worked with in other patterns, however. Mark strips on the fabric the width of the template (which includes seam allowances) and then use the template to mark the shapes. This method has been diagrammed several times. The trapezoid with only one triangle cut away must be cut of fabric with all the layers stacked right-side-up and the template must not be turned over but used in the position shown. Otherwise the fabric pieces will be reversed. This will not occur with the other trapezoid.

Your diagram must be followed carefully to be sure you use the right block in the correct position when chain-sewing them for the top.

"Lanterns in the Night," Pattern 84, Illus. 132, evolved from Pattern 38, a sketch in Chapter 3. The block is made by piecing four sets of strips from which segments are cut (Step 1). Two segments of one strip are pieced end-to-end to one segment of another to form the two different rectangular blocks (Step 2). The scale of the design appears rather large in the drawing, but this is not necessarily true, because the scale is adaptable to your choice.

When marking the strips for the sets on the fabric be sure to mark the length of the segments on the strips for the middle of the set at the same time because it is wider.

Chain-sew the segments to form the blocks. Then chain-sew the pieced blocks with setting blocks of the same size and shape (Step 3). This is an easy pattern to sew and it is attractive with the length of the blocks running either crossways or lengthwise. Turn the page around to see the effect.

"Sarah's Choice," Pattern 85 shown in Illus. 133 is another design that can be made to run horizontally or vertically. It, too, developed from the lantern pattern series in Chapter 3.

One of the blocks for this design is the same as those for "Lanterns in the Night." The other is made of the same sets of strips (Step 1), but the segments are cut only ⅓ as wide (Step 2).

Sarah Harrison, my sister-in-law, made her

Piecing diagram for "Lanterns in the Night."

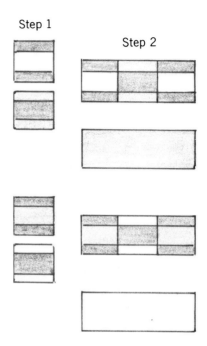

Step 1

Step 2

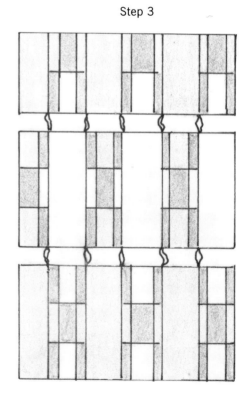

Step 3

Illus. 133, Pattern 85. "Sarah's Choice."

Piecing diagram for Illus. 133, Pattern 85.

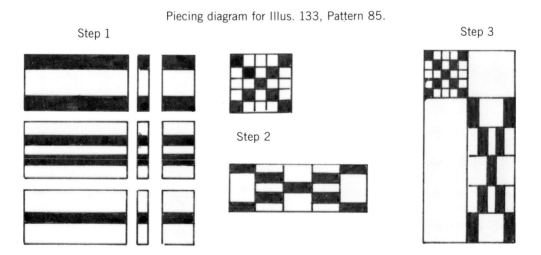

quilt with two fabrics only. She chose a deep blue-grey pattern for the small squares (1″ or 2.5cm) and narrow rectangles which form the grillwork design. The other is a cotton and synthetic blend printed in a small pattern of muted colors which coordinated beautifully with the deep blue. She strongly advises the use of 100% cotton for narrow strips, such as are used for this pattern. The soft fabric of blends created difficulties in cutting strips and also in sewing, even for a person as expert in sewing as Sarah is. She machine-quilted the printed area with a pattern of "concentric" diamonds. In spite of the problem mentioned, she is very pleased with the results of the project.

Pattern 86 (Illus. 134) is one I drew early in my quilting experience. I named it "French Ribbon Twist" because it reminded me of the lovely ribbons my mother used to pin in my hair when I was a little girl. I planned to make the bands of twisted ribbon each in a different color combination of two narrow solid color strips bordering a print strip (preferably little flowers in a row). It is difficult to find just the right fabrics for this sort of thing, so I am still collecting them.

Some years after all this began I came across an old border pattern called (you guessed it!) "Ribbon." Mine is a little different, however, because of the strip-piecing for the ribbon.

"Star and Cross I," Pattern 87 (Illus. 135) is an eight-point star enhanced with strip-piecing so that a cross is formed in the center by the strips. To make the pattern pieces, fold a paper square 10u × 10u along all the dashed lines shown in Step 1.

Cut out a paper pattern of the two triangles. Mark and cut the fabrics for these by the methods in Chapter 4.

Piece a set of strips (Step 2) 2u wide plus seam allowances. Press the seam allowances on half the sets in one direction and on the other half in the opposite direction.

Make a template (Step 3) of the diamond shape and use it to mark half the sets. Turn the template over to mark the other half of the sets.

Add a small triangle to one *end* of each diamond as in Step 4. Add a large triangle to one side of the diamond as shown in Step 5 to form a triangular group. Piece pairs of these triangles to make square units. Then join four units as shown in Step 6 to complete the block. Naturally you know by now to chain-sew wherever possible.

At this point I stopped for lunch. The pattern I had been describing was still taped to my drawing board for easy reference while I wrote. Now I sat across the room from it and this distance made a difference in the appearance. I could not help noticing how much the spaces left between the squares re-

Illus. 134, Pattern 86. "French Ribbon Twist."

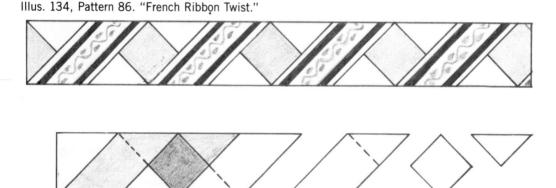

Step 1. Draft pattern and make pieces.

Step 2. Piece, mark and cut Set 1.

Step 3. Piece squares and triangles.

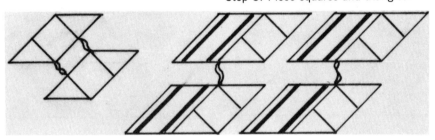

sembled lattices separating blocks. I could imagine how they would look if these spaces were actually shaded strips with a dark square at the crossing. I liked the idea so much that I wanted to share this variation with you, so I shaded in the strips and made the center square dark. Then I drew small diagrams of Step 6 to replace the larger drawing.

This new block "Star and Cross II" should be pieced with setting blocks or with lattice 2u wide. Otherwise the blocks coming together will look quite different and the strips and square I added will really be lattices. That would be all right, too, but then the block would have chevron points at the corners and a large square in the center. Draw it as a diagram that way, also. You may like it.

Pattern 88 shown in Illus. 136 is another design with eight points this time made with four flags around a center square—hence the name, "Four Flags."

Step 1 shows the diagram for folding the paper to make the three pattern pieces needed. The square and the triangle are cut from fabric by methods described in Chapter 4.

Construct the trapezoidal pieces by the instructions in Pattern 69, Variation 2 in Chapter 4.

Steps 3, 4, 5 and 6 show the piecing order for constructing the block.

"Two Pinwheels," Pattern 89 (Illus. 137) developed from "Rail Fence" which is Pattern 66, Illus. 95 in Chapter 4. Two pinwheels are to be seen when the blocks are pieced together. The dominant pinwheel is emphasized by a pieced strip. A tiny pinwheel forms as the corners of the block meet.

Unit measurements are given in Step 1 for all pieces. Make a template of Piece 4 and measure it across at the arrows (see Step 4) for the measurement of the strips. Sew and press these and then mark them as shown in Step 2. Step 4 shows the making of the pattern for the long triangle. Half-rectangles are marked and cut in the same way as half-triangles in Chapter 4.

Follow Steps 3, 4, 5 and 6 to construct the squares. Then chain-sew four squares together to make the block.

Mark and cut the triangles by the method for half-squares in Chapter 4. Then follow Steps 4, 5 and 6 to construct the blocks.

Illus. 135, Pattern 87. "Star and Cross" (I and II).

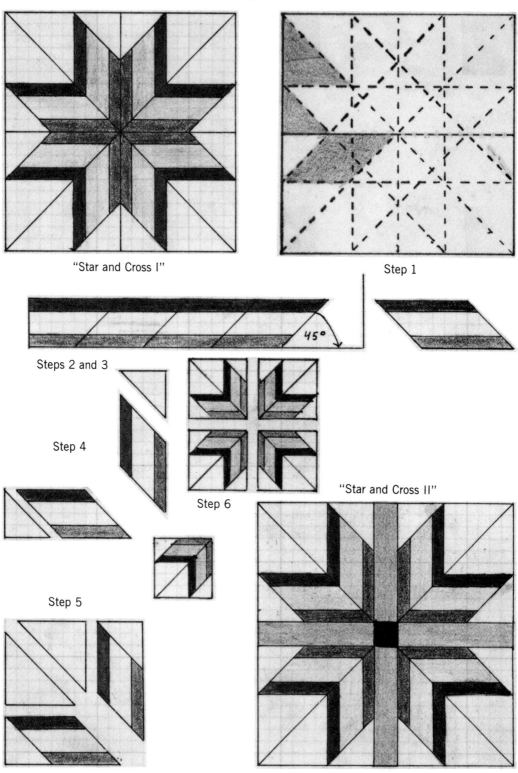

"Star and Cross I"

Step 1

Steps 2 and 3

Step 4

Step 6

"Star and Cross II"

Step 5

45°

130

Illus. 136, Pattern 88. "Four Flags."

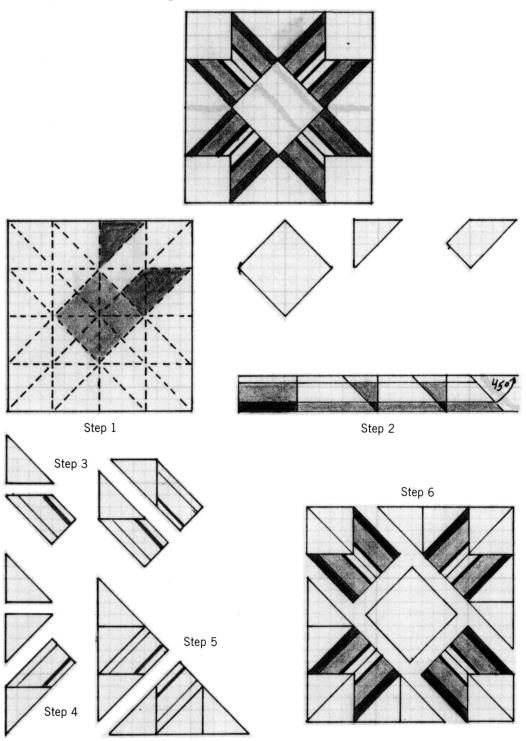

Step 1

Step 2

Step 3

Step 4

Step 5

Step 6

Illus. 137, Pattern 89. "Two Pinwheels."

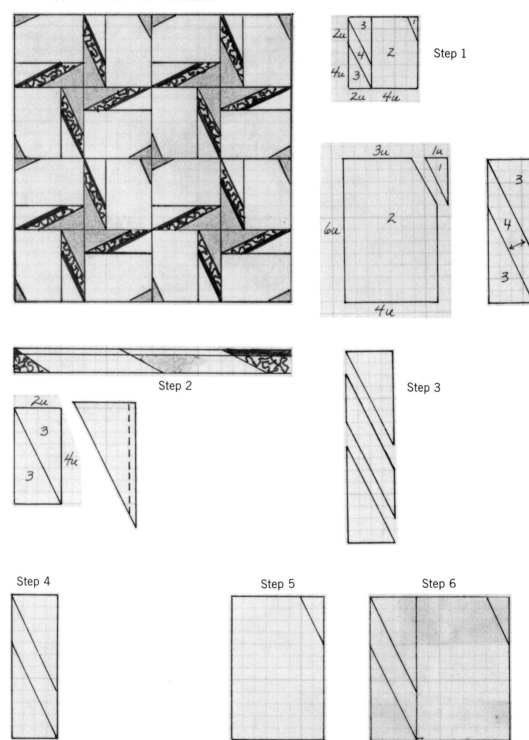

Step 1

Step 2

Step 3

Step 4

Step 5

Step 6

"Rockford Square," Pattern 90, Illus. 138, is a nine-patch variation. The side patch is similar in appearance to a pair of segments for a chevron band, but the construction is a little different to save fabric.

Step 1 shows folding the paper square to make the pattern pieces in Step 2. The width for the strip is measured across the diamond shape where it is creased by one fold as seen in Step 2. The fabric diamonds are made in the same way as those for Illus. 135, Pattern 87 (Step 3).

Illus. 138, Pattern 90. "Rockford Square." Block shown on following page.

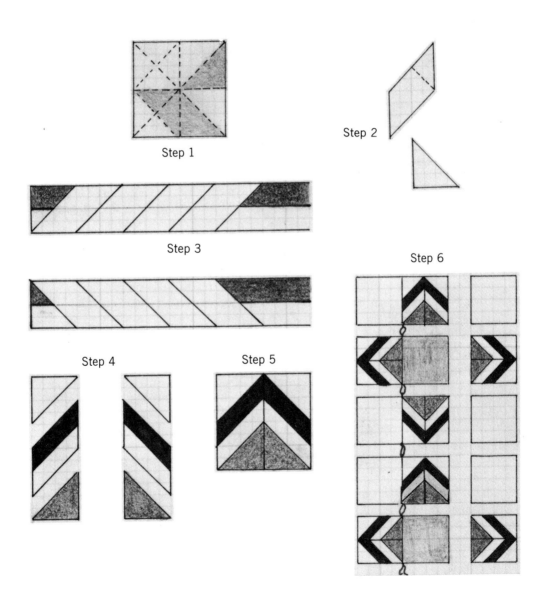

Step 1

Step 2

Step 3

Step 4

Step 5

Step 6

133

"Rockford Square"

"Chatelaine and Medallion," Pattern 53 (Illus. 139), was seen in Chapter 3. Two blocks are used alternately to form the design. The first is a nine-patch variant that resembles an "Irish Chain" block. Instead of the setting block usually used with that pattern I have used a medallion design. No dark square is pieced at the corners of this block so there is a gap in the chain there.

The diagram for an alternate version of the medallion block is included.

For each block, segments are cut of three-strip sets and pieced to make small nine-patch blocks. These are pieced with setting patches to make the two larger nine-patch blocks used alternately to form the design.

"Variations on a Patch" (Pattern 54, Illus. 140) is not as complicated as it might appear to be at a glance. The design is divided into four different nine-patch blocks each of which is subdivided into smaller nine-patches.

A diagram of the top must be made and followed at each step. I have drawn diagrams of each block of pieced and plain squares showing all the three-strip segments in order as they are used. With this information constructing the blocks is simply a matter of chain-sewing. Follow this diagram every step of the way to form the four-block. Then follow your own diagram of the top to make sure of choosing the correct block and of stitching it in the appropriate position to fit the pattern. Like many other complicated appearing things, when this is approached step-by-step it is really quite simple.

Several years ago I designed this block of interlocking squares with a small square to fill in two opposite corners. Not long ago I discovered a Seminole pattern of two squares in the same arrangement. In that pattern the bands of the squares are wider than mine and no small squares fill in the corners.

When four of my blocks are pieced with a narrow lattice it is easy to see why the design is called "Square Dance" (Illus. 141, Pattern 91). Enough squares are included in my drawing to show the complete relationship of the blocks in their various positions. The pieced border I designed for the pattern is included on three sides. The light border is 2u wide the same as the lattice. The dark border is 3u wide. All other unit measurements are given with the piecing diagram.

Illus. 139, Pattern 53. "Chatelaine and Medallion."

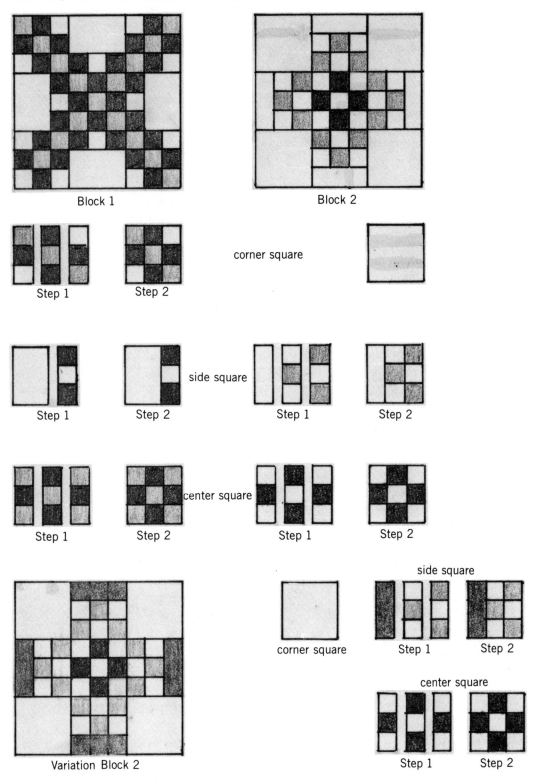

Block 1

Block 2

Step 1   Step 2   corner square

Step 1   Step 2   side square   Step 1   Step 2

Step 1   Step 2   center square   Step 1   Step 2

Variation Block 2

corner square

side square

Step 1   Step 2

center square

Step 1   Step 2

Illus. 140, Pattern 54. "Variations on a Patch."

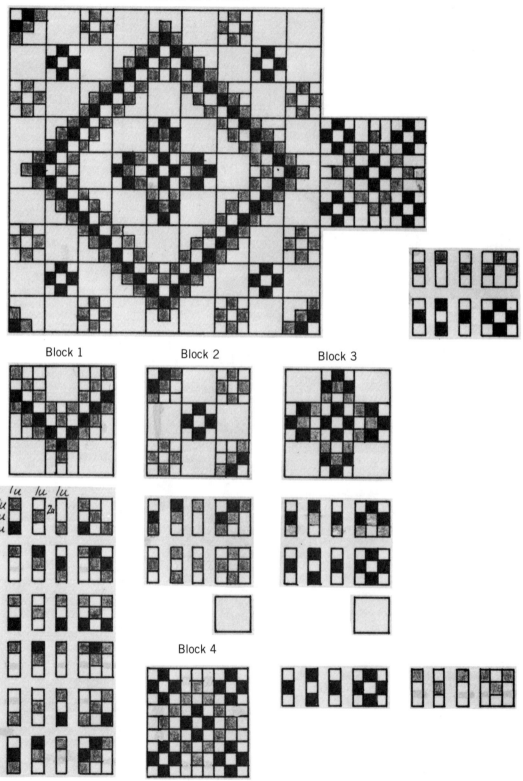

Block 1 Block 2 Block 3

Block 4

Illus. 141, Pattern 91. "Square Dance."

Illus. 142. Piecing diagram for "Square Dance."

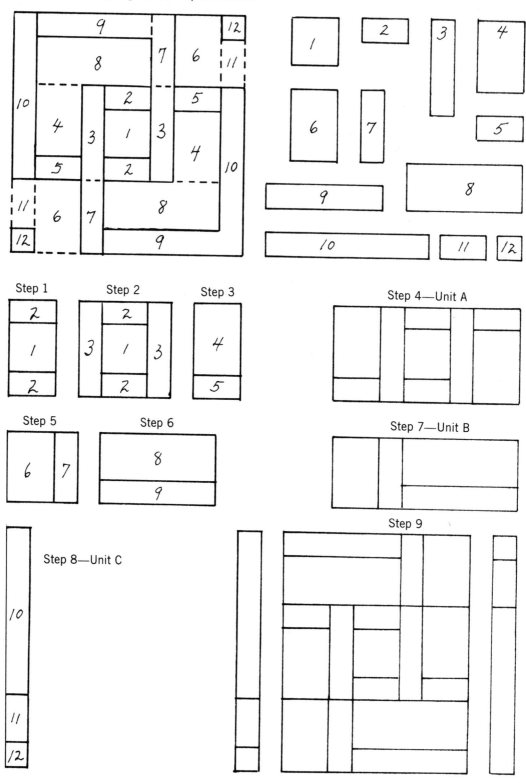

Illus. 143, Pattern 92. "Dance of the Bumblebee."

My husband named the next quilt "Dance of the Bumble Bee" (Illus. 143, Pattern 92). In this design, two zigzag bands of segments are set with simple plain bands. The first drawing shows the quilt in the variation for a double bed. The second diagram shows all the information for the piecing. Even though the pieces in the segments are only 1″ (2.5cm) wide, the shortest *seam* sewn for the band is 5½″ (14.0cm), a length easily handled by anyone who sews.

At the top right of the diagram is a drawing of the zigzag band showing all the pieces (a). b is a drawing of the corner section of segments. In c is shown a sequence of three groups of segments to show how the band joins the corner and how the sections repeat to form the band.

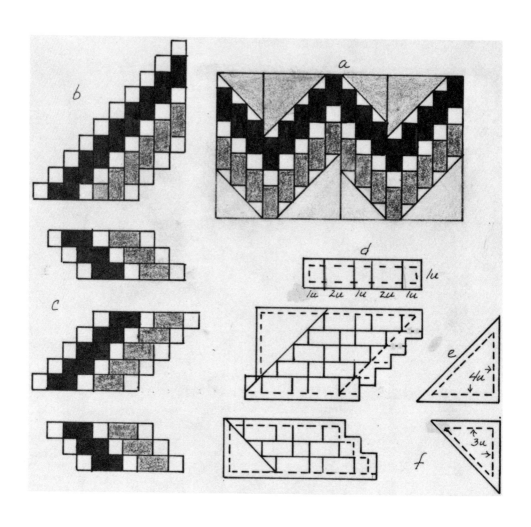

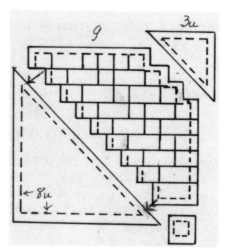

Illus. 144. Piecing diagram for Pattern 92.

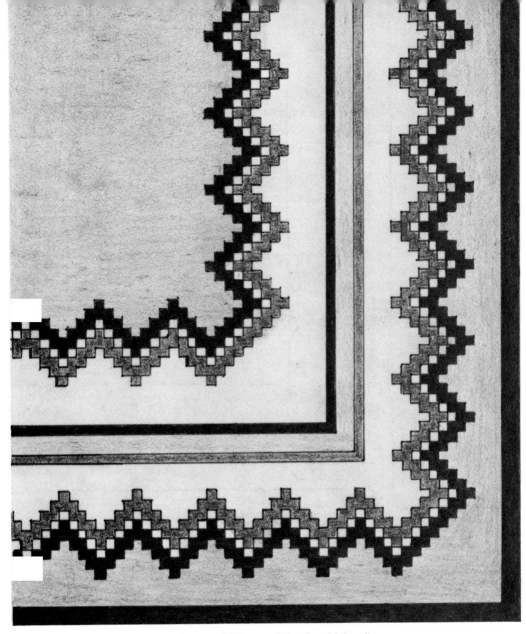

Corner of "Dance of the Bumblebee."

In d is a single segment with seam allowances. Under it is a diagram of the piecing of a five-segment section, and the way triangles are added to it to fill in the zigzag of the band (e).

Notice that this triangle is stitched to only four of the segments. The end of the fifth segment is part of the edge of the band. Study a to see how this works.

Part f shows the piecing of the three-segment section and how to add the triangles.

A diagram of the piecing of the corner section is seen in g. A few pieces have been removed from a few of the lower segments to fit the shape needed for the corner as seen in the lower right part of the drawing. An extra square is added below the last partial segment to fill out the pattern there. Then the triangles are pieced across the opposite corners to make the square corner of the border.

Obviously the size of quilt needed to fit beds of differing size will affect the proportions of the bands and borders. The following information is the instructions for adapting this design to spreads and coverlets for various bed sizes.

The unit-measurement scale for these quilts is 1u = 1″. Measurements given here for these quilts are *before* quilting. Remember that the quilt shrinks during the process, and the amount of shrinkage is related to the amount of quilting done. To make any of these quilts a little larger or smaller, change the width of the outside border beyond the band.

In order to adjust the two bands of segments to fit the various sizes of quilts, some variations in the borders and center were necessary. Therefore not all the sizes will look exactly alike. Each size does place one band of segments on the top of the mattress and parallel to the edges of it on both sides and the foot. Another band is located near the outside edges of the quilt.

If a smaller quilt than is included in this group is desired, it is best to change the scale so that 1u = ¾″ (1.9cm) or 1u = ½″ (1.3cm). This is because the larger scale would not fit well into a smaller area as the design is planned. If you prefer to work with the larger scale it is possible to leave off the outside band from any size quilt to make it smaller that way.

To begin, draw a complete diagram of the size quilt you plan to make. Let one square of the graph paper = 1″ (2.5cm) of the quilt. This will likely require taping several sheets of paper together. If possible use graph paper which has 8 or 10 (shown) squares to the inch to keep the diagram small. Draw a line down the middle of the diagram to represent the middle of the quilt. This line should not be drawn on a line of the graph paper but down the middle of a line of squares so that you can start with the segment which is in a point position when drawing the bands.

Next mark a U-shaped line to represent the edge of the mattress. Extend the arms of the U up far enough beyond the mattress measurements to allow for making the quilt long enough to go over the pillows and to tuck under if you like it that way. I usually allow at least 8″–12″ (20.3–30.5cm) for this.

Now you are ready to begin drawing the segments of the band to fit into your mattress top. The following information is given to help you in your planning. *Add seam allowances to all measurements.*

Twin spread (86″ × 104″ or 215 × 260cm)
The center will be 23″ × 72″ (58.4 × 180cm) of a light-medium fabric.
The center band will have 3 dark "points" across the end × 9 dark "points" long (+ 4 segments to finish the repeat).
Measure the length of each border to fit.
The first border will be 4″ (10.2cm) wide (shown white).
The striped border will have two 1″ (2.5cm) stripes with a 2″ (5.1cm) stripe between.
The third border is 3″ (7.6cm).
The outside band will have 8 × 12 (no extra segments) light points.
A 4″ (10.2cm) border (light-medium) is added outside this band, and there is no room for a dark border, too. If you want a dark edge, bind the quilt with dark fabric.

Double-bed coverlet (86″ × 96″ or 215.2 × 240cm)
Shorten all bands by 8 segments. Otherwise make this size the same as the twin spread.

Double-bed spread (98″ × 104″ or 245 × 260cm)
The center will be 31″ × 72″ (78.7 × 180cm)
The center band will have 4 dark points across, 9 dark points (+ 4 segments) long.
All borders are the same widths given for the twin spread.
The outside band will be 9 × 12 light points.

Queen coverlet (94″ × 112″ or 235 × 280cm)
Make the same as for the double coverlet except that the center and all borders will be 3″ (7.6cm) longer and 1 repeat (8 segments) is added to the end of each border.
Then increase the width of the outside border to 5″ (12.7cm) and add a 2″ (5.1cm) dark border beyond that all around the entire quilt.

Queen spread (108″ × 120″ or 270 × 300cm)
The center rectangle will be 31″ × 80″ (78.7 × 200cm).
The center band will be 4 × 10 dark points (+ 4 segments).
The first border is 4″ (10.2cm) wide.
The striped border is 4″ or 10.2cm 1″ (2.5cm) + 2″ (5.1cm) + 1″ (2.5cm) wide.
The third border is 7″ (17.8cm) wide.
The outside band will have 10 light points across and 13 light points (+ 4 segments) long.
The fourth border is 3″ (7.6cm) wide.
Beyond that add a 2″ (5.1cm) dark border all around the quilt.

King coverlet (108″ × 108″ or 270 × 270cm)
The center rectangle will be 31″ × 72″ (78.7 × 180cm)
The center band will have 4 × 9 (plus 4 segments) dark points.
The first border is 4″ (10.2cm).
The striped border is 4″ (1″ + 2″ + 1″).
The third border is 3″ (7.6cm).
The outside band is 10 × 12 light points.
The fourth border is 3″ (7.6cm).
Then add a 2″ (5.1cm) border around the entire quilt.

King spread (122″ × 122″ or 305 × 305cm)
The center rectangle will be 31″ × 80″ (78.7 × 200cm).
The center band will be 4 × 10 points (+ 4 segments).
The first band will be 4″ (10.2cm).
The striped band will be 4″ (1″ + 2″ + 1″).
The third band will be 7″ (17.8cm).
The outside band will be 11 × 13 (+ 4 segments) dark points.
The fourth border will be 4″ (10.2cm).
Then add a 4″ dark border around the entire quilt.

"Oriental Screen" is a design in which all the piecing is done in the wide lattices (Illus. 145, Pattern 93). The blocks are plain, offering an opportunity for a display of fine quilting.

If you prefer a more conventional piecing, the pattern can be made as a block having unpieced squares (4u) to fill in the corner areas. This block could be set with lattice to achieve more or less the same effect. The difference would be that there would not be the large unpieced area for quilting.

On a scale of 1u = ½″ (1.3cm), the block would be 14″ (90.3 sq. cm) square. This is a nice size for a pillow. Whether pieced as blocks or lattice, four of the patterns arranged in a square would make an attractive wall hanging.

You have, of course, recognized in this design my familiar little three-piece strip. It is pieced into a square and a rectangle to form the pattern. If this is to take the form of a lattice, a rectangle the same size as the pieced one is used to separate the designs. This would measure 4″ × 6″ (10.2 × 15.2cm) on the scale mentioned above (1u = ½″ or 1.3cm). The square setting block on this scale would be 12″ (30.5cm).

The next design, Pattern 94 (Illus. 146), is my setting of "Rail Fence" which I call "Fence Around the World." This particular piece is a wall hanging. The pieced area is 26″ square (167.7 sq. cm). With a scale of 1u = ½″ (1.3cm), each narrow strip of the block has a finish width of ½″. Without the method of using segments of a set of four strips for the piecing, this would be a very tedious and time-consuming job. Be sure to mark the segment length when marking the strips on two fabrics. Lay the unmarked fabric which is to be sewn to these under them and sew before you cut. Then cut strips only and sew them to the other pair to complete each set. Press the seams before cutting the segments.

The narrow dark border, as shown, allows the design to make its own statement like a melody played or sung without any accompaniment. You may prefer a wider border, perhaps even one of two or three strips, to frame and enhance the piece.

"Celebration Star," Pattern 95 (Illus. 148) was originally designed as a round Christmas

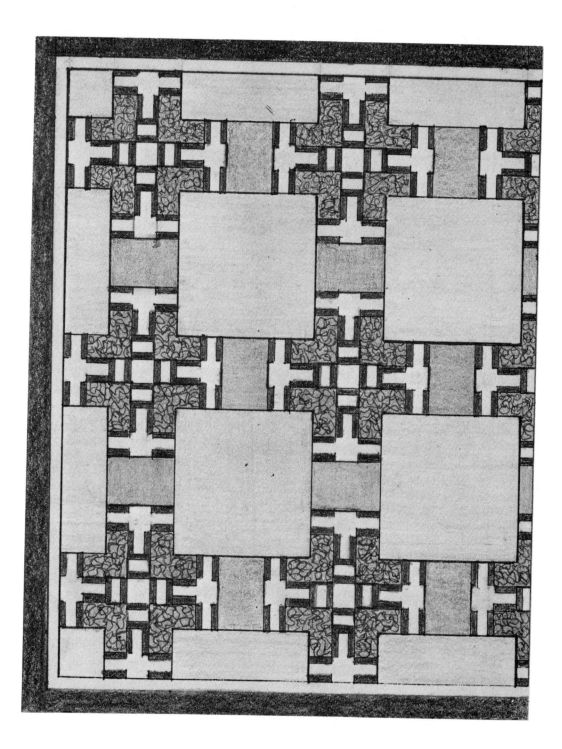

Illus. 145, Pattern 93. "Oriental Screen."

Block 1   Block 2

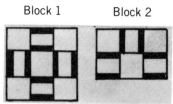

Illus. 146, Pattern 94. "Fence Around the World."

tree skirt and therefore had a hole in the middle. Some years later I saw a block of a similar design printed on a paper of patterns. Eventually I made the square wall hanging which is seen on the cover of this book. On the back of the piece I have stitched a strip along the top for a brass curtain rod to slip through. A silk cord fastens to the ends of the rod for a hanger. When a strip of fabric is used for a casing of this type, it should always be of a fabric which matches the back.

Since I have chosen this type of support for my hanging, nothing shows beyond the edges. This makes it more versatile to use. It can also serve as a cover for a small table or a centerpiece for a large one. It can be laid over the back of a chair for color in a room or even be used as a lap robe.

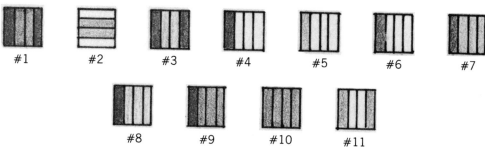

| #1 | #2 | #3 | #4 | #5 | #6 | #7 |

| #8 | #9 | #10 | #11 |

Illus. 147. Piecing diagram for Pattern 94.

Illus. 148, Pattern 95. "Celebration Star."

The star design itself can be used in other ways as well. It can, for example, be the medallion for a quilt with various borders surrounding it. On a smaller scale it could be blocks for a quilt, a pillow top or such.

Admittedly this is not an easy pattern to piece by the usual methods as I found out when I first attempted it in working with the design for the Christmas tree skirt. I tried various methods of putting the pieces together. First I drafted all the pieces precisely and began sewing one to another. I found it necessary to be very particular about matching the ends of the stitching lines. Even then, when I would open out a pair of stitched pieces to press them, the ends were sometimes still very reluctant to lie flat and in line across the ends. Since I was planning to use the design for a class, I knew I had to find a better way.

I tried string-piecing the pieces over paper to hold the ends in place during piecing. Later the ends could be cut off in line. This part worked well, but the paper was awkward to work with and then there was all that paper to be torn out. Little bits of it were left clinging to the stitching. I didn't like this solution.

Then I tried cutting strips of measured length and devised a marked card to be used as a guide in off-setting each successive strip end in relation to the last for stitching. A template was made and laid over the pieced strips to mark the exact shape of the half-diamond wedges. Pairs of wedges were then stitched and afterwards the ends of the strips were cut off. Generally speaking this worked quite well except that some students ironed the wedges out of shape after they were accurately pieced. (I had to be careful not to do this, myself.) When that happened the wedges were no longer the same size. So when they were marked with the template the pieces would not cross the shape in the same places and thus would not match at the points when cut that way. Fortunately this was obvious before cutting because the ends of the strips would not match when pinned for sewing. Even when no problem developed from careless ironing, some people had problems sewing the wedges without stretching them.

"Celebration Star" was also sewn for use as a tablecloth or a wall hanging. In this version there is no hole in the middle, so all the wedges come together at the center. The points must be very precisely pieced to achieve an accurate meeting. This is another piecing challenge even for the most experienced piecers. Some people have difficulty because of stretched seams or inaccurate seam widths.

What I needed was a method of controlling all these potential difficulties. I finally worked out the following method which solves all problems. If you are an accomplished piecer and take pleasure in your skill in handling the most difficult situations by the traditional methods, you may not be interested in this method. It does require a little more fabric and also a fairly inexpensive tearaway interfacing (the soft type) so it costs

a little more. But if you are eager to make this design and you have problems with the usual methods, you may want to try this method. I will begin the explanation with the drafting of the pattern, which is much the same for any piecing method.

Make a paper square and fold or mark with a ruler all the *dashed* lines shown in Illus. 149A in the order indicated by the numbers. Each new line divides in half the distance between folds or lines already made, and each passes through the center of the square. When all the dashed lines have been transferred to your paper, then draw or fold the solid lines in the diagram on your own paper square to complete the shapes needed for the pattern pieces.

I have lettered the shaded pieces for easy reference. Not all are needed for piecing, since you may either set in the squares and triangles between the points of the star or divide them in half and sew one-half to each half-diamond, after it is pieced. Sixteen half-diamonds are required for the star.

Illus. 149. Piecing instructions for Pattern 95.

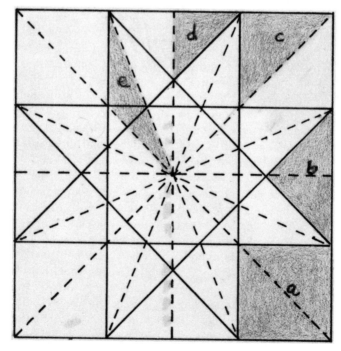

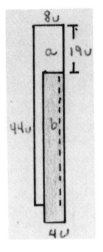

Step 1

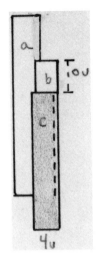

Step 2

Left half of diamond

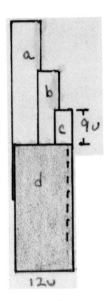

Step 3

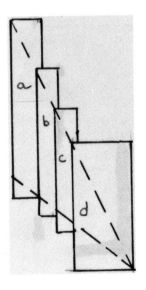

Step 4

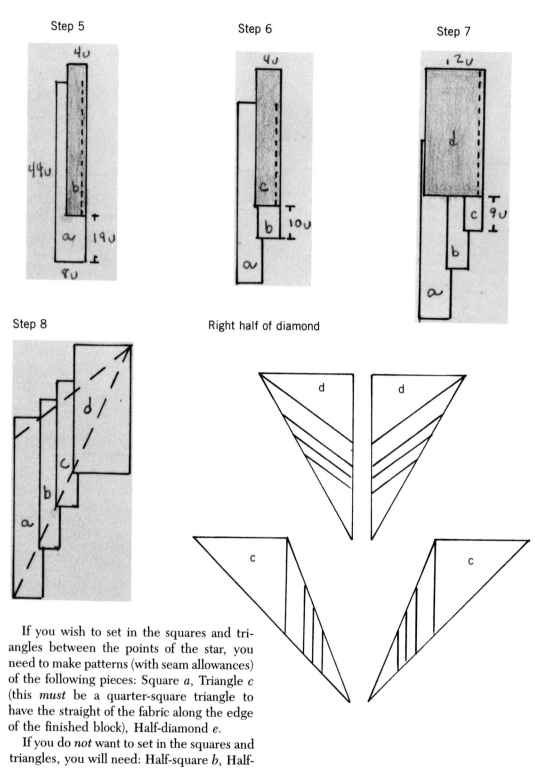

Step 5

Step 6

Step 7

Step 8

Right half of diamond

If you wish to set in the squares and triangles between the points of the star, you need to make patterns (with seam allowances) of the following pieces: Square *a*, Triangle *c* (this *must* be a quarter-square triangle to have the straight of the fabric along the edge of the finished block), Half-diamond *e*.

If you do *not* want to set in the squares and triangles, you will need: Half-square *b*, Half-square *d*, and Half-diamond *e*.

You will need a template of the half-diamond shape, including seam allowance. This is used for marking the shape on the strips pieced for the half-diamond. If you use tearaway interfacing, mark the pieces on the interfacing, too. Mark squares and triangles directly on the fabric.

The construction method for this design is a variation of sewing a set of strips. Cut strips of fabric by the following measurements and divide them into the indicated lengths:
Strip *a* is 8u wide; cut pieces 44u long.
Strip *b* is 4u wide; cut pieces 36u long.
Strip *c* is 4u wide; cut pieces 30u long.
Strip *d* is 12u wide; cut pieces 32u long.

For the left half of the diamond, lay Strip *b*, right sides together, along the right edge of Strip *a* and 19u down from the top end of the strip, as shown in Step 1. Sew a ¼" (.6cm) seam. Lay Strip *c* right sides together on Strip *b* and 10u down from the end and stitch the seam (see Step 2). Lay Strip *d* on Strip *c* 9u down from the top and sew as shown in Step 3.

Gently press, *not iron*, the seams being careful not to stretch the pieces out of shape. Then lay the half-diamond template on the wrong side and mark the solid cutting lines (Step 4). Do not mark the stitching lines.

For the right half of the diamond, Strip *b* is placed on Strip *a* so that the lower end is 19u up from the bottom end of Strip *a* as in Step 5. Strip *c* is placed 10u up from the end of Strip *b* as in Step 6. Strip *d* is placed 9u up from the end of Strip *c*. See Step 7.

Press gently as before, and mark the cutting lines as shown in Step 8.

Make eight of each half-diamond. Then lay one of each half together along the long side, which will be joined to form the diamond. Match the strip seams carefully and pin them together on the *stitching line*. Sew a ¼" (.6cm) seam, tiptoeing over the pins so that the seams do not shift. Check the points formed by this seam before trimming. Make eight diamonds this way. When sewing the half-diamonds to form the diamonds, the stitching must not extend into the seam allowances, but *must* stop where one stitching line touches the next, where they come to-gether at the star's center. Gently press all seams in the same direction.

If you have chosen *not* to set in squares and triangles between the points, now is when you should add Triangles *b* and *d*. Check your diagram to be sure to add the correct triangle to the outside points of the diamonds so they can be stitched together to form a square.

To join the diamonds, match the edges along the cutting line and pin the strip seams along the stitching line. Then carefully pin the edges (some will be bias) of the half-squares which complete the seam. Stitch a ¼" (.6cm) seam, taking care not to stretch it. Two diamonds, correctly joined, as in the diagram, will form a square. Four of these, stitched in the correct position complete the star in a square.

If you wish to *set in* squares and triangles between the points, first join the pieced half-diamonds and then the diamonds, remembering *not* to stitch into the seam allowances, where the points meet at the center. Press as before. Set in the squares by the methods shown in Illus. 105, Pattern 70.

If you want to use tearaway interfacing as an aid, purchase the soft type. Use the half-diamond template to mark the shapes on the interfacing. Cut one for each half-diamond to be made. Then piece by the methods described, but stitch the pieces over the interfacing. This stabilizes the shapes during the entire process. Don't tear away the interfacing until the star is completed and pressed and the squares and triangles added. Then tear gently along the stitching lines, holding the interfacing with both hands. If there has been inaccuracy in piecing the seams, they may not match exactly. If the difference is slight, gently tear the interfacing along the two seams for about 1" (2.5cm) to free them. Then pin them exactly together and the ends of the strips will ease flat. Pin the interfacing to the fabric on each side of the tear.

If there is too much difference between the matching of the seams to correct in this way, you must resew the piece even if it means removing other pieces to do this. (See Chapter 1 for instructions on ripping.)

Illus. 150. Pattern 95 set with lattice.

When all corrections have been made, pin the two pieces together all along the seamline and trim away any extra fabric beyond the interfacing. Sew a ¼" (.6cm) seam.

Borders, as desired, can be added to the star whatever its scale, to make a piece the size you want.

If the pattern is drafted in a size appropriate to use as a quilt block you may like the setting diagram included here (Illus. 150).

The pieced lattices set the stars a little apart but the way they are pieced, with strips to match the different fabrics used for the corners of the blocks and the half-squares at the sides, also ties the whole top together as a unit.

One other piece of information may be helpful to some. If you want to make this pattern but feel that you are not quite ready to tackle the piecing of all sixteen seams as they come together at the center, you can avoid doing them by piecing a circle in the middle of the star. First draw a small circle in the center of your paper pattern before you make the diamond pattern. This way you will piece a diamond with a hole in the middle. Staystitch the hole. Draw a circle on fabric to match piece d. Add ¼" (.6cm) all around for a seam allowance Staystitch just inside the drawn circle and baste the seam under with small stitches. Small stitiches make a smoother circle. Snip the seam allowance almost to the staystitching so it will lie flat. Pin a piece of fabric or interfacing under the hole in the star and slipstitch the circle over the hole, also covering the staystitching.

If you want to make a Christmas tree skirt draft your star and then fill in between the points with curved pieces rather than with squares and triangles. Make the hole in the center and bind or turn in the edges. Leave one seam between diamonds unstitched to allow the skirt to slip around the tree trunk. (A pattern with complete instructions for this skirt is available.)

Another way to use this pattern on a small scale is to make a pillow top or a small piece for a table center. Matching placemats can be made of half-stars. These pieces are excellent ways to practice the piecing of the design on a small scale.

Illus. 151. "Celebration Star" with circle in center.

In Conclusion

Strip-piecing in one form or another is being explored at present by various people. It is seen in everything from "new" variations on the "Log Cabin" theme to the most contemporary of abstract quilting. In this book I have applied it in a more traditional spirit to patchwork piecing in general. In spite of this some of the designs look very contemporary.

In Chapter 2 we examined the methods created by the Seminoles to piece the tiny, intricate designs with which they adorn their clothing. I included along the way some variations which I use. Suggestions were made for developing variations of the patterns shown. The thought was suggested that to become familiar with these methods and to think about piecing from this approach can be a source of ideas. It is also a direction which might be followed for further exploration.

Additional ways of encouraging the development of ideas was discussed in Chapter 3. As an example of my own ways of doing this, I followed two different lines of design, as they developed. They also showed how the patterns which developed were influenced by the concepts of string-piecing and would not likely have emerged outside that approach to piecing.

In Chapter 4 I discussed the advantages of a knowledge of a variety of methods from which to select when doing patchwork piecing. I explained in detail the basic methods which I use, also sharing several variations of methods which I developed in my own piecing and teaching. As examples of these methods and of their application, numbers of patterns were diagrammed, and step-by-step instruction shown.

The use of Seminole patterns in the piecing of quilts was explored in Chapter 5. The methods employed for making quilts with these designs were discussed and diagrams drawn to show the way those patterns would look when pieced as quilts.

Chapter 6 includes an assortment of designs with piecing instructions. Some were first mentioned in Chapter 3 and are here shown for piecing. Some are simple patterns and some more difficult. Some depend upon the fast and easy methods found in this book to make them practical to piece. All have been patterns which I have enjoyed sharing with you in this special way.

As I came to the end of my first book I experienced a feeling of accomplishment and of a gentle sadness that, for me, always accompanies endings. I also looked forward to new growing and learning experiences and new opportunities for sharing the things that I enjoy.

Since that time I feel that I have had these kinds of experiences. The writing of this book has, itself, been one of them. The fact that it presents me with an opportunity to share again with old friends and with new ones, as well, is a special source of pleasure to me.

So it is that I invite you to turn again with me, to all the tomorrows which stretch out ahead, filled with opportunities and challenges beyond our dreams.

METRIC EQUIVALENCY CHART

MM—MILLIMETRES   CM—CENTIMETRES

INCHES TO MILLIMETRES AND CENTIMETRES

INCHES	MM	CM	INCHES	CM	INCHES	CM
⅛	3	0.3	9	22.9	30	76.2
¼	6	0.6	10	25.4	31	78.7
⅜	10	1.0	11	27.9	32	81.3
½	13	1.3	12	30.5	33	83.8
⅝	16	1.6	13	33.0	34	86.4
¾	19	1.9	14	35.6	35	88.9
⅞	22	2.2	15	38.1	36	91.4
1	25	2.5	16	40.6	37	94.0
1¼	32	3.2	17	43.2	38	96.5
1½	38	3.8	18	45.7	39	99.1
1¾	44	4.4	19	48.3	40	101.6
2	51	5.1	20	50.8	41	104.1
2½	64	6.4	21	53.3	42	106.7
3	76	7.6	22	55.9	43	109.2
3½	89	8.9	23	58.4	44	111.8
4	102	10.2	24	61.0	45	114.3
4½	114	11.4	25	63.5	46	116.8
5	127	12.7	26	66.0	47	119.4
6	152	15.2	27	68.6	48	121.9
7	178	17.8	28	71.1	49	124.5
8	203	20.3	29	73.7	50	127.0

YARDS TO METRES

YARDS	METRES	YARDS	METRES	YARDS	METRES	YARDS	METRES	YARDS	METRES
⅛	0.11	2⅛	1.94	4⅛	3.77	6⅛	5.60	8⅛	7.43
¼	0.23	2¼	2.06	4¼	3.89	6¼	5.72	8¼	7.54
⅜	0.34	2⅜	2.17	4⅜	4.00	6⅜	5.83	8⅜	7.66
½	0.46	2½	2.29	4½	4.11	6½	5.94	8½	7.77
⅝	0.57	2⅝	2.40	4⅝	4.23	6⅝	6.06	8⅝	7.89
¾	0.69	2¾	2.51	4¾	4.34	6¾	6.17	8¾	8.00
⅞	0.80	2⅞	2.63	4⅞	4.46	6⅞	6.29	8⅞	8.12
1	0.91	3	2.74	5	4.57	7	6.40	9	8.23
1⅛	1.03	3⅛	2.86	5⅛	4.69	7⅛	6.52	9⅛	8.34
1¼	1.14	3¼	2.97	5¼	4.80	7¼	6.63	9¼	8.46
1⅜	1.26	3⅜	3.09	5⅜	4.91	7⅜	6.74	9⅜	8.57
1½	1.37	3½	3.20	5½	5.03	7½	6.86	9½	8.69
1⅝	1.49	3⅝	3.31	5⅝	5.14	7⅝	6.97	9⅝	8.80
1¾	1.60	3¾	3.43	5¾	5.26	7¾	7.09	9¾	8.92
1⅞	1.71	3⅞	3.54	5⅞	5.37	7⅞	7.20	9⅞	9.03
2	1.83	4	3.66	6	5.49	8	7.32	10	9.14

Index